Guide to
Taking up
a Franchise

The Daily Telegraph

Guide to
Taking up
a Franchise

THIRTEENTH EDITION

Colin Barrow,
Godfrey Golzen
and Helen Kogan

KOGAN
PAGE

First published in 1983
Thirteenth edition 1999

Kogan Page Limited
120 Pentonville Road
London N1 9JN

'He' and 'his' have been used throughout for convenience only, though 'she' and 'her' apply equally in most cases. In fact, there are more women employed in the franchise industry than men.

Throughout the term 'franchisor' will be used to refer to a business which grants a licence or a franchise to another person for use of its trade name, trademarks and business system.

British Library Cataloguing in Publication Data

A CIP record for this book is available from the British Library.

ISBN 0–7494–2919–4

Typeset by Saxon Graphics Ltd, Derby
Printed in the United Kingdom by Creative Print and Design (Wales), Ebbw Vale

Contents

Contents

THE 'PERFECT' OPPORTUNITY

Before long the British will eat as many pizzas as the Americans – three times as much as now.

That's the prediction of Perfect Pizza – a franchise specialist that leads the way in the rapidly expanding take away and home delivery market.

The company has over 200 stores nationwide and is looking for more franchisees to join the network. The plan is to open 100 new outlets during the next five years.

Recruitment takes place from both sexes and a wide range of ages and ethnic backgrounds, but successful applicants are all focused, dynamic and hands-on operators.

Several franchisees have up to five stores under their control and the more mature operations can turnover £350,000 per annum. Indeed, a Perfect Pizza franchisee will see a return on investment in just three years – and that's considerably faster than industry standards!

The advantages are well documented – a High Street brand name, realistic business projections, practical training based on years of experience, a full support package and a sound track record.

Franchise Director, Martin Clayton, explains: "We look for people who want to succeed. They need to be hungry, even a little greedy. Profit isn't a dirty word in our business."

Perfect PIZZA

THE UK'S LARGEST PIZZA DELIVERY COMPANY

The Perfect Franchise

Do you want to control your own destiny and gain financial rewards with the security of a well established brand?

Are you prepared to work hard with a 'hands on' approach, rise to continual challenges and new opportunities?

If yes read on

Perfect Pizza is the UK's No.1 pizza delivery company with 200 stores throughout the UK. We are looking for enthusiastic business partners like yourself now!

Quality product

The finest ingredients are used to make our famous range of pizzas and side orders which are augmented by continuous innovation.

Start up

Our experts will help with site selection, store design, staff recruitment, purchase of equipment and legal matters.

Operations back-up

Experienced Regional Managers will assist with the everyday running of your store to help realise your investment.

Marketing support

Comprehensive support from our experienced Marketing Team at both a local and national level.

Staff training

We will provide extensive start up and on-going training for both you and your staff.

Centralised purchasing and distribution

Bringing you value and quality, combined with quick and efficient deliveries.

If you have a minimum of £35k liquid cash to invest, contact Martin Clayton on 01932 568000.

Or write/fax: Franchise Sales, Perfect Pizza, The Forum, Hanworth Lane, Chertsey, Surrey KT16 9JX.

Fax: 01932 570628.

PREVIOUS WINNER FRANCHISOR OF THE YEAR

PREVIOUS WINNER FRANCHISOR OF THE YEAR

Introduction

Arriving at the airport, having spent the previous night at a *Holiday Inn*, Mr Smith goes to the *Budget Rent a Car* office to pick up a car since his was out of action the day he left home. He goes straight to his office, where his secretary has typed up the copy for some promotional leaflets. A hundred of these are to go out to his Midlands sales office and he takes them round to *Prontaprint* to be printed up. There is no time to send them through the post, so he takes them round to *Business Post*, who operate a fast delivery service.

On the way back to his office, he stops at a *Tie Rack* shop to buy a scarf for his secretary to thank her for staying late to finish the work. He then phones home, where his wife tells him that she has been discussing redecorating the sitting room with *Colour Counsellors* and also that she has been looking at new shoes for the children at *Clarks Shoes*.

For his part Mr Smith has been asked by his wife to look in at *Snappy Snaps*, the film processing service, where he might as well see if the photos from their summer holiday are ready. Mr Smith has a lot of paperwork to catch up with before he sets off for home, though. Rather than go out for lunch, he asks an office junior to pop round to *McDonald's* and bring him a takeaway. It will come in a box so he can eat it at his desk without causing too much mess for the cleaners from *Safeclean* to deal with when they come round in the evening. His wife has also been getting a quote to do a thorough spring clean from an agency called *ServiceMaster*.

Each service or outlet referred to in the morning's activities is a business format franchise and he could probably fill a large part of his week using one or other of the 587 types of business. Body Shop is scarcely 20 years old and the whole franchise concept spread only slowly in the decade after the first really major British franchise, Wimpy, got going in the mid 1950s.

Since then, however, development has been very rapid; more rapid, perhaps, than most people realise because, until you look at the names and details of franchises given on pages 204–17, you may not have been aware that some of these firms are franchises at all. It is a fair bet that if you look at your local High Street or shopping centre with that list in your hand, you will find several business format franchises in operation. This is especially true of London and the South-East, the South-West, North-West, West and East Midlands which are the main regions for franchising activity. London and the South-East account for 32 per cent of all franchise units, but it is significant that the distribution is becoming more even. The London and South-East share has gone down from 42 per cent over the past five years, while Wales, Scotland and Northern Ireland have seen an upturn.

According to the latest annual franchise survey produced by the National Westminster Bank and the British Franchise Association, the number of franchised units has risen over the past year to 29,100, representing big overall growth since the beginning of the 1990s. The turnover of the industry over the past year – up by 9.4 per cent to £7 billion, is well over the rise in inflation over this period.

At a time when there is universal concern about employment, franchising presents a positive picture, if in a modest way. The number of people employed in it, directly and indirectly, is estimated to be 222,700. But the size of the franchise sector depends how you define it. There are signs that the boundaries of franchising are extending in this country towards franchising petrol stations, property management, delivery services, recruitment, training and certain limited legal areas, such as will-writing. There is also a view that the arrival of self-assessment in the preparation of tax returns will offer big opportunities in personal tax preparation as an alternative to going to a firm of accountants, as has happened in the USA. If these trends continue and franchising becomes defined in some of the broader terms indicated in Chapter 1, it could become a really major player in the services market, as is already the case in the USA where it accounts for 12 per cent of retail sales alone.

So is this a band wagon you should jump on without further delay? Well, it depends. There is general agreement that you shouldn't go into franchising purely as an alternative to unemployment, though some of the shakier franchise propositions are aimed precisely at this market. In that connection you are advised to pay close attention to the chapters on Asking the Right Questions, Financial Viability and Evaluating Yourself, which chart some of the pitfalls awaiting the naïve, the unwary and the over-optimistic. However, franchising is a positive step into self-employment, particularly for those with business experience but no actual experience of running a business – often the case with those who are looking for something to do following a corporate career. Significantly, 80 per cent of those who go into franchising do so because they want to go into business for themselves. Only 20 per cent give 'redundancy' as a prime factor.

Franchising operates in a way that takes some of the sting and isolation out of going it absolutely alone. We will deal with this aspect in more detail in Chapter 5. The most compelling reason of all, however, for the growth both of franchising and interest in it as a way of going into business is its success. It is reckoned that as many as 70 per cent of all new businesses fail, whereas 90 per cent of new franchises succeed. That they sometimes succeed because it is in the interests of the franchisor to pull out all the stops to prevent them from failing – so it is said – is an argument in their favour rather than against. It helps to be able to turn to someone who will not only be there to advise you, but in whose interests it is to do so, because, clearly, the difficulties of an outlet have to be resolved by the franchisor. Otherwise it reflects on his whole operation. No wonder, then, that when regular employment is diminishing, taking up a franchise looks like an attractive alternative for someone who has money to invest in running his own business.

However, while franchising eliminates some of the more costly and at times disastrous bumps in the learning curve of working for yourself, it is not an easy way to riches either. Furthermore, there are stresses and dangers as well as advantages in some of the compromises it offers between self-employment and working for someone else. Some of these could be exploited by unscrupulous operators who tend to emerge whenever there are inexperienced people around with money to invest in business ventures. Though some of the less savoury versions, or rather perversions, of franchising are now subject to legislation – pyramid selling, for instance – it is quite possible for an unscrupulous franchisor to stay within the law and give the franchisee very little in return for his fee. This book has been written, not only to tell intending franchisees what exactly franchising is, how it operates and who the main franchisors are, but also to alert them to the pitfalls. They can be avoided if you ask the right questions. Once you have signed on the dotted line and parted with your fee, though, it is too late to turn back and the person who is wise before the event rather than after it is in an infinitely better position. To impart some of the necessary wisdom is the object of *Taking Up a Franchise*.

Priority Management

Priority Management is an international training and development organisation - our main focus is helping individuals and team to maximise and measure their productivity and effectiveness. We continue to expand, with more than 300 franchises in 18 countries, including 26 UK offices. Our programmes are used in over 500,000 companies worldwide.

The Priority Management business creates revenue from:

- Personal productivity and management training - helping people attain a higher level of achievement in both their personal and professional lives.

- Our unique diagnostic tool - measuring and identifying skill levels at individual, team and organisational level.

- Consulting services and public speaking

- Repeat product sales

We deliver a wide range of training programmes, tool and processes designed to improve individual and organisational productivity.

As a new franchise owner you receive intensive training to meet your initial and on-going needs as you grow your business. This starts with a month of owners training, focusing on proven and sophisticated sales skills and facilitated workshop methods. You will also receive initial telemarketing support to help you get started. We will attend sales appointments with you and deliver your first workshops.

As you launch your Priority Management business you will be:

- Consultatively selling your training programmes/tools and their substantial benefits to business and organisations.

- Facilitating interactive workshops

- Providing one-to-one coaching after each workshop. This enhanced learning is your most valuable competitive edge over other management training.

- Administering repeat trainings, materials and accessories sales.

For more information please contact:

Rachel Truelove
Network Development Director
Priority Management
Oakwood, Spa Road
Melksham, Wiltshire SN12 7TA

Tel: 01225 709 533
Fax: 01225 702 902

RIBBON REVIVAL: A dynamic company

In just five years of operation, Ribbon Revival has been voted the fastest growing company in its market sector and has emerged as one of the franchise industry's leading success stories of the Nineties. This dynamic company has so far established over 45 branches in the UK and overseas, servicing some 40,000 customers, including such household names as British Airways, BP and Sainsbury, as well as a number of national and local government departments worldwide.

REPUTATION

However, with a reputation for constant evolution, Ribbon Revival does not intend to sit back on its laurels. A number of exciting new developments, responding to current market trends, have recently been announced to move the company forward into its next stage of growth.

Ribbon Revival is in the process of re-branding itself as a printer specialist, although the core business is to remain in printer consumables. Robin Le Prevost, business development manager, explains "Setting up the company as a franchise operation has allowed us to develop centres of technical excellence, with each of the franchisees playing an important role. They bring that expertise to the door of the customer and get to know the customer personally, giving them the opportunity to build upon the service they supply. A direct result has been that we are now servicing and maintaining printers as well as providing consumables."

PARTNERSHIPS

In order to achieve this and retain a reputation for quality service provision, business partnerships have been set up with industry leaders such as Hewlett Packard, Epson, Brother and Kyocera. Ribbon Revival has also become an authorised agent for HP and secured distribution rights for the others, allowing franchisees to sell new printers in addition to consumables.

This expanding product line has attracted a growing interest from aspiring franchisees overseas, in particular the Middle and Far East. "There seems to have been a realisation that our product line and set-up provide a credible opportunity for anyone wishing to run their own business," confirms Robin. "Although in the UK, with the upturn in the economy engendering a drop in redundancies and the resultant feeling of greater employee security, franchisee recruitment has become more difficult. We have reacted quickly to this change in market situation though, introducing a number of new measures to assist potential franchisees."

Ribbon Revival's initiatives have produced a more flexible package which can be matched to the skills and resources of the aspiring franchisee. For instance, the licence fee now incorporates stage payments for a territory, enabling the franchisee to start in a smaller territory with options to expand over time.

A knock-on effect of the ability to start with a smaller territory is that working capital can be reduced safely. Added to this, in its wish to find the right applicants, Ribbon Revival is itself prepared to look at joint ventures, whereby the company supplies some of the capital required.

GROWTH

The growth in the range of Ribbon Revival products and services has also had an impact on start-up costs, particularly where the equipment package is concerned. Consequently, Ribbon Revival has gone back to basics in its franchise package offer. The franchisee can then buy into the enhanced package as their business grows and resources become available.

"The result of these initiatives is that the ingoing cost for new franchisees can be reduced by over 50%, making the whole undertaking much more attractive," concludes Robin Le Prevost. "But one of the most important benefits is that these measures have not compromised the level of training we provide. Our training programme is intrinsic to the success we have achieved to date and we fully intend to continue our rate of growth over the next five years."

For further information on the business opportunities available, contact Mik Underdown on Tel: 01481 729552 or Fax: 01481 729554.

Everyone Loves To See Their Name in Print

The Personalised Book Company, offers a unique business opportunity, which caters to this desire. Software packages are available, which are designed to produce, in just a few minutes; Personalised Books, First Names Analysis, Surname History, The Day You Were Born, Pet Pedigree and Personalised Clocks. Prices are from £149.00 to £1295.00.

Personalised Books

Imagine the joy of a small child, who becomes the star of the story and is part of the action with his or her favourite super hero. The reaction of children, reading these books is amazing, which is why they have become so popular, parents love them, and will reorder time and time again. Best Personalised Books, based in Dallas, are constantly seeking to expand their range of books, adding new titles every year. In 1998 'SPIDERMAN' 'X-MEN' and 'THE THREE LITTLE PIGS' were released, expanding the Super Hero range, which already includes Batman, Superman and Power Rangers. In August 1998 THE LITTLE MERMAID and BEAUTY AND THE BEAST were released. No other personalised Book Company can boast such prestigious and popular titles, which almost sell themselves.

First Names Analysis, interprets the meaning of over 14,500 first names, including the origin, personality traits and even lucky lottery numbers!! In the same program a name can be made into a personalised poem, or two names can be placed side by side for weddings and anniversaries.

Surname History, has a database of over 200,000 surnames from all over the world. This package can print out professional and attractive illuminated scrolls, detailing early origin, history, dates, names and places, together with a written description of Coats of Arms.

The Day You Were Born, details the events, holders of high office, sporting winners and even a cost of living comparison on a birthday, anniversary or other important milestones.

Personalised Clocks, using pre-printed backgrounds, text is printed onto a clockface and then inserted into the clock, making a useful and individual gift, which can be made in minutes.

Pet Pedigree, prints a certificate for a cat or a dog, with a brief description of the animal, and includes the name of the pet, the owners name and has a place for a photograph.

All these software packages can be purchased separately or as a complete package. The products can be purchased for Birthdays, Christmas, Anniversaries and many other occasions. They can be sold on site, in shops, shopping centres or craft fairs, or by mail order and party plan, or through hospitals, schools and nurseries.
The only limitation to selling these delightful products is your own imagination!

Part One:

Is Franchising For You?

1 | **What Franchising Means**

FORMS OF FRANCHISING

We have referred in the Introduction to business format franchising. This is the form of franchising operated by such well-known names as Wimpy, Prontaprint and Body Shop and is in fact what people generally now mean by the word. There are, however, other forms of franchising and it is important to be clear about the distinctions between them. The term franchise covers a wide variety of arrangements under which the owner of a product, a process, a service or even just a name having certain connotations (eg that of a sportsman) licenses another to make or use something in exchange for some form of payment. This can be either direct, in the form of a fee and/or a royalty, or indirect in the shape of an obligation to buy a service or product in which the licence holder has some kind of commercial interest. An example of the latter with which most people are familiar is the 'tied' pub, where the licensee has to obtain his supplies from a particular brewery. This type of arrangement, by the way, has been around for some 150 years, so franchising in the UK has a history stretching back a long way before the Wimpy bar.

Let us look at the various types of relationship between licensee and licensor which are also described as franchises but which, though having a good deal in common with the business format franchise, are also quite different from it.

The latest BFA survey points out, incidentally, that if some of these forms of franchising were to be considered as part of the total sector – as is the case in the USA – the total value of annual sales in the UK would be in the order of £60 billion; accounting for 35 per cent of all retail sales.

1. *A distributorship* for a particular product, such as a make of car. An arrangement where both parties are legally independent, as vendor and purchaser, except that the purchaser, in exchange for certain exclusive territorial rights, backed up by the vendor's advertising, promotion and, possibly, training of his staff, will be expected to hold adequate stock and maintain his premises in a way that reflects well on the vendor's product or service.

2. *A licence to manufacture* a certain product within a certain territory and over a given period of time, have access to any secret process this involves and use its brand name in exchange for a royalty on sales.

3. *The use of a celebrity name* to enhance the sales appeal of a product and guarantee, at least by implication, its quality. The most common example is the endorsement, by a sports personality, of equipment associated with his activity and bearing his name, in return for a royalty payment by the manufacturer.

BUSINESS FORMAT FRANCHISING

Although all these forms of franchising continue to flourish, business format franchising has emerged as the dominant and most rapidly expanding mode. Its main features are:

1. It is a licence for a specific period of time to trade in a defined geographic area under the franchisor's name and to use any associated trade mark or logo. In 1989 EC regulation No 40 87/88, commonly known as the Franchise Block Exemption, came into force. This allows qualifying franchisors to include in their agreements provisions that would normally fall foul of Article 85 of the Treaty of Rome. That article covers restricted trade, price fixing and creating exclusive territories.

2. What is franchised is an activity, usually some form of service,

which has already been tried and tested to produce a formula of operating that has been found to work elsewhere.

3. The franchisor provides the entire business concept of that formula (usually called the 'blueprint') for the conduct of operations. This must be followed by the franchisee. In fast food, for instance, the ingredients of any 'secret' recipes for the type of food being offered are strictly laid down, as are the specifications for the surroundings in which it is served.

    The blueprint is generally set out in an operating manual which is given to the franchisee when negotiations are completed.

4. The franchisor educates the franchisee in how to conduct the business according to the method laid down in the blueprint.

5. The franchisor also provides back-up services in order to ensure that the franchise operates successfully. This should certainly cover advertising and promotion of the franchise's name in general and may also cover promotion of the particular franchise in its locality. It can cover many other aspects: ongoing business advice including help in raising finance, market research into the viability of a particular location for trading purposes, assistance with negotiating leases and obtaining planning permissions, site development, the provision of building plans and specifications, a standard accounting system – virtually anything connected with setting up a new business.

6. In exchange for the business blueprint and the services the franchisor provides, the franchisee is expected to make an initial investment in the business and to pay a weekly or monthly royalty to the franchisor thereafter, normally based on turnover. There may also be an obligation on the franchisee to buy some or all goods and equipment from sources nominated by the franchisor. When the franchisor benefits financially from such an arrangement, acting in effect in the role of a wholesaler, the royalty will be lower. In some cases, in fact, there may be none at all.

7. The participation of the franchisor in setting up the business does not mean that he owns it. It belongs to the franchisee and he is free to dispose of it, though he will probably have to give the franchisor first refusal and obtain his approval of the

person the business is sold to, if the franchisor does not want to take it off his hands.

Types of business format franchise

Job franchises

These require a financial investment in the £7000–£20,000 range and could be described as 'buying a job' – however, with back-up in the way of training, customer leads, advertising etc from the franchisor. Suitable for someone with little capital but having a specific area of expertise or willing to be trained in it, eg cleaning or vehicle repair and maintenance services.

Business franchises

These require a higher level of investment, typically in the range of £70,000–£120,000 in stock, equipment and premises. There are large numbers of business franchises available in such areas as retailing, food services and business services such as High Street printing shops.

Investment franchises

Here you are talking about initial investments of over £120,000. Hotels and some of the larger and more established fast food outlets come into the top range of this category at around £750,000.

Definition of a franchise

A formal definition of a franchise is set out by the British Franchise Association, as follows:

A contractual licence granted by one person (the franchisor) to another (the franchisee) which:

a) permits or requires the franchisee to carry on during the period of the franchise a particular business under or using a specified name belonging to or associated with the franchisor; and

b) entitles the franchisor to exercise continuing control during the

---

> period of the franchise over the manner in which the franchisee carries on the business which is the subject of the franchise; and
>
> c) obliges the franchisor to provide the franchisee with assistance in carrying on the business which is the subject of the franchise (in relation to the organisation of the franchisee's business, the training of staff, merchandising, management or otherwise); and
>
> d) requires the franchisee periodically during the period of the franchise to pay to the franchisor sums of money in consideration for the franchise or for goods or services provided by the franchisor to the franchisee; and
>
> e) is not a transaction between a holding company and its subsidiary (as defined in Section 154 of the Companies Act 1948) or between subsidiaries of the same holding company or between an individual and a company controlled by him.

The last clause establishes the important distinction between a franchise and an agency; though this official definition is certainly useful, it does not mention a number of aspects which are important from the point of view of the person taking up a franchise. It does not indicate that an initial fee is usually payable by the franchisee nor does it stress that the subject of the franchise should be a tried and tested commercial operation (though running a pilot scheme is a condition of membership of the BFA). It does not mention, further, that the business, once set up, is the property of the franchisee, nor does it warn him of the degree of control he may be subject to under clause b). Further, it gives no indication of the extent of the back-up services that the franchisee might reasonably expect to get for his money. In other words, the definition is not an adequate measure against which to check the franchise contract, a subject we shall deal with in more detail in Chapter 8.

The British Franchise Association expects its members to follow its code of practice, set out below.

> 1. **BFA Code of Practice** shall be based on that established by the Advertising Standards Association and shall be modified from time to time in accordance with alterations notified by the ASA. The BFA will subscribe fully to the ASA Code unless, on some

specific issue, it is resolved by a full meeting of the Council of the BFA that the ASA is acting against the best interests of the public and of franchising business in general on that specific issue; in this case the BFA will be required formally to notify the ASA, setting out the grounds for disagreement.

2. No member shall sell, offer for sale, or distribute any product or render any service, or promote the sale or distribution thereof, under any representation or condition (including the use of the name of a 'celebrity'), which has the tendency, capacity, or effect of misleading or deceiving purchasers or prospective purchasers.

3. No member shall imitate the trade mark, trade name, corporate identity, slogan, or other mark or identification of another franchisor in any manner or form that would have the tendency or capacity to mislead or deceive.

4. Full and accurate written disclosure of all information material to the franchise relationship shall be given to prospective franchisees within a reasonable time prior to the execution of any binding document.

5. The franchise agreement shall set forth clearly the respective obligations and responsibilities of the parties and all other terms of the relationship, and be free from ambiguity.

6. The franchise agreement, and all matters basic and material to the arrangement and relationship thereby created, shall be in writing and executed copies thereof given to the franchisee.

7. A franchisor shall select and accept only those franchisees who, upon reasonable investigation, possess the basic skills, education, personal qualities and adequate capital to succeed. There shall be no discrimination based on race, colour, religion, national origin or sex.

8. A franchisor shall exercise reasonable surveillance over the activities of his franchisees to the end that the contractual obligations of both parties are observed and the public interest safeguarded.

9. Fairness shall characterise all dealings between a franchisor and its franchisees. A franchisor shall give notice to its franchisee of any contractual breach and grant reasonable time to remedy default.

10. A franchisor shall make every effort to resolve complaints, grievances and disputes with its franchisees with good faith and good will through fair and reasonable direct communication and negotiation.

The ethics of franchising

The BFA's code of practice is actually contained in a more far-reaching document, an explanatory guide available from the Association, entitled _The Ethics of Franchising_. It is intended to lay down ethical standards for members, but at the same time the BFA hopes that these standards will also be followed by non-members.

The BFA has laid down that franchisors should disclose the following subjects to franchisees in the literature they send them or that they should otherwise be prepared to commit themselves to stating them in writing:

☐ the business and financial position of the franchisor;
☐ the personnel involved in the franchise company;
☐ the franchise proposition;
☐ the franchisees already operating;
☐ the financial projections and the contract.

The document goes on to explain what is meant by 'fair dealing' and, perhaps most important of all, describes the arbitration procedures available in the case of a dispute between franchisors and franchisees. These can also be applied through the BFA acting as an intermediary when the franchisor is not a BFA member – but it should be stressed that arbitration can only be used to resolve a dispute if both parties agree to do so. Once they do and make an application to the BFA for an arbitrator's intervention, his findings when he has heard both sides of the case are legally binding under the Arbitration Act. You cannot, in other words, appeal against them in a court of law. However, arbitration is a lot cheaper than legal action.

The BFA is, of course, a franchisor organisation and in the main the code of ethics is aimed at member companies. However, its existence in itself gives some further protection to franchisees, irrespective of whether the franchisor with whom you are negotiating is a BFA member, because it sets standards to which any reputable franchise will be expected to adhere by the banks and the legal profession. Any franchisor who does not meet its requirements should be looked at with misgiving.

The practice of business format franchising

According to the 1998 NatWest/BFA survey the numbers of franchise systems outside the dairy sector are:

Retailing	106
Commercial and industrial services	81
Direct selling, distribution etc	78
Catering, hotels	65
Building services	47
Vehicle services	39
Cleaning services	27
Employment agencies, training	24
Parcel, courier and taxi services	21
Estate agents, business transfer agents	20
Quick printing, copying, graphic design	12

These systems are also in the top bracket of the number of units in operation, though there is no indication of the average turnover per unit. That is a pity, because although the number of units in each system is a sign that it is doing well, the significant criteria are turnover and profitability per unit.

Overall, the picture on both turnover and profitability looks encouraging. Ninety per cent of franchisees report they are trading profitably, though the number of those claiming high levels of profitability has fallen slightly in the last year, indicating that margins may be coming under pressure. Hard work, good customer service, a good product, sensible pricing and providing value for money are given as the main reasons for success. Negative factors are generally attributed to the state of the economy as a whole, or to local economic problems rather than to lack of support from franchisors.

Taking up a franchise is a question of judging the economic climate as much as the merits of the system itself. The simplest form and usually the cheapest to acquire is a job franchise service which is run from home – a cleaning service, for instance, or a vehicle maintenance franchise such as Hometune. Much the largest group of franchises, though, are those which entail acquiring premises and often a substantial investment in equipment in addition to the initial fee payable to the franchisor: fast food restaurants and print shops are two of the most visible and widespread franchises of this type. At the top end of the market are investment franchises like Holiday Inn, where the start-up costs can run into seven figures. A prime Wimpy bar franchise will now also run to over £700,000. Overall the range of activities which can be franchised is very wide and some 65 have been identified in the USA, going from hotel ownership at the top end to a soft drink bottling franchise with the unlikely name of Cock 'n' Bull Ltd at the other. The latter is an indication that not all American enterprises can be readily transplanted to the UK (an important point to consider if the franchise is of foreign origin, incidentally), but there are at the moment at least 40 types of franchise in Britain, covering a variety of fields from fast food to dry cleaning.

The principles in each case are broadly the same and it might at this stage be useful to take a hypothetical example from the fast food area – one of the most active ones – to illustrate them from the point of view of both franchisee and franchisor.

A basic operation

Let us use as an example a fast food operation offering slimmers' lunches. They already own a couple of outlets for which they have found a catchy name – Calorie Countdown – and for which they have established a standard image in terms of decor, layout, tableware and graphics. They have a gimmick; each dish at a counter service buffet has a calorie rating, and along with your bill you get a calorie count for what you have bought. They also have some recipes and dishes which they have pioneered. They are doing well at both outlets, have ironed out the start-up bugs, and learnt a lot about the catering and accounting problems involved in running first one and then a second restaurant of this type.

The indications now are that there is a demand for a similar place on the other side of town. It's a tempting prospect, but there are two problems. One is that of control; their existing outlets are within walking distance of each other and so control is at present easy, but it will be a different matter with the third outlet which will be some distance away. How can they get someone motivated and experienced enough to run it without close supervision? The other problem is financial and administrative. Even if such a person is available – a member of their existing staff, for instance – do the owners of Calorie Countdown have the capital to invest in another outlet and do they want to get involved in further wage bills and administrative overheads, even though the indications are that success is probable? If they are doubtful whether this is the right way to expand, the answer could be to franchise the Calorie Countdown business format.

As we have seen, this consists of a business concept which is both original and has been tested and found to work in practice (though in this case an adviser might feel that, since the firm in question is opening up its first franchise, this fact ought to be reflected in the financial arrangements), which has some secret recipe or process, which has a degree of standardisation in design terms and which has acquired enough of a reputation with the public for a demand to arise from another location. Further, in terms of the definition of a business format franchise, the owners of Calorie Countdown would give an undertaking not to let anyone else trade under that name within an agreed radius, would pin-point a location for the franchise, help the franchisee to get permission from the planning and environmental health departments, possibly make a presentation to the bank for finance, get decorators, graphic designers and architects to have the new Calorie Countdown look as much like the original as possible and come to some agreement about the extent and nature of advertising. While this was going on, they would be training the franchisee to prepare food the Calorie Countdown way and teaching him about all the administrative matters he will have to deal with and advising him on procurement of equipment and supplies. Finally, all the operating instructions would be embodied in a manual and someone from the original Calorie Countdown would be on hand to keep an eye on the franchise in its opening weeks.

In exchange for all this, the franchisors of Calorie Countdown would expect the franchisee to pay them a start-up fee and some continuing form of payment, either by way of a royalty on sales or profits, or through an agreement to purchase food or equipment from them; or possibly some combination of all these factors.

What we have described is a very basic operation. The more sophisticated packages offer a wide range of services which include:

☐ assistance from head office staff in negotiating site acquisition and development;

☐ celebrity openings;

☐ annual training sessions in the latest merchandising techniques;

☐ regular assistance with financial and administrative matters and/or formal procedures for dealing with these;

☐ on demand 'trouble shooting' and so forth.

The better established and stronger the franchisor, the more services he will offer in his package – but the more costly, in general, the franchise will be.

2 Advantages and Disadvantages of Taking up a Franchise

The advantages and disadvantages of taking up a franchise depend to some extent on the content of the agreement but there is a core of balancing factors which are largely common because they relate to the nature of the kind of activity which franchising involves.

THE FRANCHISOR

From the franchisor's point of view, the *advantages* are that he does not have any direct investment in an outlet bearing his name. The inventory and equipment are owned by the franchisee. Because of the shortage of prime sites, there is a growing trend for franchisors to acquire leases on behalf of franchisees or at any rate to stand as guarantors. Nevertheless, the effect on the liquidity of the franchisor, in contrast to expansion by opening branches, is enormous – though if he does his job properly there are heavy start-up costs in piloting the franchise and in setting up and maintaining training. Thereafter there are further costs in providing a continuing service to franchisees in such matters as research and development, promotion, administrative back-up and feedback and communication within the network. The expectation is that these costs will be offset by the fact that:

☐ the franchisee, as the owner of the business, is more likely to be highly motivated than an employee and more responsive to local market needs and conditions;

☐ the franchisor receives an income from the franchise;

☐ he saves on personnel and administrative costs; and

☐ without direct financial involvement, he may in this way derive some of the benefits of expansion, inasmuch as franchising gives him economies of scale from centralised purchasing and, if he wishes it and it is feasible, some degree of centralised administrative facilities.

The *disadvantages* are that, although the failure of an individual franchise may reflect badly on the franchise operation as a whole, all he can control is the format itself and he can only influence the running of individual operations by pulling the reins on this or that clause in the agreement – the broad terms of which we shall discuss shortly. In extreme cases he may terminate the agreement or at any rate not renew it, but he cannot throw the franchisee out as if he were an employee. He is therefore dependent on the willingness of the franchisee to observe the rules and play the game, while at the same time any failure to do so is equally and perhaps more damaging to the franchisor (and to other franchisees) than to the franchisee concerned because of its adverse effects on the franchise as a whole.

Another disadvantage sometimes turns out to lie in the curious mixture of dependence and independence that franchising produces. The franchisee is encouraged to think of himself as an independent business entity and to a large extent this is indeed the situation. Nevertheless, he is operating the franchisor's business concept under a licence for which a fee is payable. There are cases where the franchisee identifies so closely with the particular business he is running that he ultimately resents the payment of the fee. The success is felt to be due to the franchisee's efforts, not to the franchise concept or to the franchisor. This is apt to be particularly so if the franchisor adopts a lower profile than he should, either in terms of direct help or in matters such as national advertising. Clearly, of course, the franchisee would be obliged to pay under the terms of the agreement, but a sour relationship is not good for either party, so it is up to the franchisor to maintain his part of the bargain both in letter and in spirit. Franchises are a matter of mutual interest and obligation.

THE FRANCHISEE

From the point of view of the franchisee, also, there are advantages and disadvantages which might, perhaps, be most clearly expressed in the form of a list.

Advantages

☐ A business format or product which has already been market tested and, presumably, been found to work; consequently, major problems can be avoided in the start-up period.

☐ A recognised name of which the public is already aware and which has credibility with suppliers.

☐ Publicity, both direct in that the franchisor advertises his product or services, and indirect promotion through signage and other corporate image promotion in all the franchisor's outlets.

☐ Although taking up a franchise is not cheaper than starting on your own, it is considered that the percentage of expensive errors made by individuals starting on their own is substantially reduced by adoption of a tested format.

☐ Direct and close assistance during the start-up period.

☐ A period of training on production and management aspects.

☐ A set of standard management, accounting, sales and stock control procedures incorporated in an operating manual.

☐ Better terms for centralised bulk purchase negotiated through the franchisor, though he may be looking for mark-ups in this area as a source of revenue from the franchisee.

☐ The benefit of the franchisor's research and development in improving the product.

☐ Feedback throughout the network on operating procedures and the facility to compare notes with other franchisees, both formally and informally.

☐ Design of the premises to an established scheme saves on interior design fees and may eliminate these altogether where the franchisor has a set of specifications.

☐ The benefit of the franchisor's advice on equipment selection and initial inventory levels, though this may not be impartial where the franchisor is also the supplier.

☐ Help with site selection, negotiating with planning officers and developers.

☐ Possibly, though not universally, access to the franchisor's legal and financial advisers.

☐ The protected or privileged rights to the franchise within a given area.

☐ Improved prospects of obtaining loan facilities from the bank.

☐ The backing of a known trading name when negotiating for good sites with letting agents or building owners.

Disadvantages

☐ Business format franchising is, of necessity, something of a cloning exercise. There is virtually no scope for individual initiative in matters of product, service or design.

☐ The royalty (sometimes called a management fee) paid to the franchisor. This is usually based on gross turnover or on profits. The problem here is that if the franchisor is not pulling his weight or if the franchisee feels this to be the case, the royalty can be the subject of bitter dispute.

☐ High turnover does not necessarily imply a highly profitable operation. If the franchisor's income is wholly or partially based on turnover, he may try to push for this at the expense of profitability.

☐ The franchisee is not absolutely at liberty to sell the franchise even though he is in many respects operating the business independently. The sale has to be approved by the franchisor, who is also entitled to vet the purchaser and charge the cost of any investigations made to the existing franchisee.

☐ Territory agreements may be difficult to enforce in practice.

☐ The franchisee, as well as paying a royalty to the franchisor, may be obliged to buy goods and services from him as well – possibly at disadvantageous rates.

☐ Though the franchisor places all sorts of controls and obligations on the franchisee to maintain the quality of his image, the scope for doing the reverse is more limited. If the franchisor's product or service gets bad publicity, this is bound to affect the franchisee adversely, and there is very little he can do about it.

☐ The failure of a franchisor may leave the franchisee with a business which is not viable in isolation.

MUTUAL DEPENDENCE

From this list of advantages and disadvantages to both parties a more detailed picture emerges of the business format franchise as a relationship of mutual dependence which allows each party to realise his strength to mutual and, at best, equal advantage. The franchisor is able to expand without further investment and, though the return is obviously lower than from expansion by ownership, he does receive an income from the franchisee as well as getting both an outlet for his product and more muscle in negotiating the purchase of materials and equipment. The franchisee, on the other hand, is able to concentrate his entrepreneurial skills at the sharp end of sales and customer service, while the administrative headaches of setting up the business are mitigated by the uniform nature of the format. By the same token he is saved, through feedback to the franchisor of the accumulated experience of other franchisees, from making the errors to which businesses are prone in their earlier and most vulnerable stages. This relationship is expressed in agreements: the purchase agreement and the franchise agreement. But before considering these, it is necessary to evaluate the franchise as a whole.

A study by Professor Russell M Knight of the University of Western Ontario illustrates the close agreement between franchisees and franchisors on the advantages of franchising – though in general, franchisees were slightly less enthusiastic.

The advantages of franchising	Franchisees in agreement %	Franchisors in agreement %
☐ You can make more money in a franchise than in an independent business	51	47

☐	A franchise is less risky than going it alone	78	88
☐	A franchise offers greater job satisfaction than salaried employment	95	82
☐	A franchise offers more independence than salaried employment	92	83
☐	A franchise offers a proven business formula	83	99
☐	A franchise offers the benefit of a known trade name	96	99
☐	You can develop a franchise more quickly than an independent business	92	86

For the most part franchisees in the UK feel that the advantages outweigh the disadvantages, as the table below shows.

Satisfaction with franchisor relationship*

	All franchisees		Time franchise held		
			Up to	3–4	
	1996	1997	2 years	years	5 years
	%	%	%	%	%
Definitely satisfactory	55	75	72	69	80
Mainly satisfactory	37	15	17	20	11
	(92)	(90)	(89)	(89)	(91)
Mainly not satisfactory	4	4	3	5	3
Definitely not satisfactory	5	6	8	6	5
	(9)	(10)	(11)	(11)	(8)

* NatWest/BFA survey 1998

Part Two:

Evaluating Opportunities

3 Asking the Right Questions

Most franchisors have discovered that the hard sell is neither in their own interest nor that of the franchisee. Successful franchising is, as we have seen, a question of mutual dependence and a franchisee who finds or feels that he has been sold a pup is not likely to be a co-operative member of the franchise family. At the same time it must be said that, with the exception of the prohibition of pyramid selling* in the 1973 Fair Trading Act, very little specific legal protection is available to the franchisee. Basically, what protection there is, is embodied in the franchise agreement but that document is subject to omissions and commissions of wording which can make a great deal of difference to the deal which is being offered to the franchisee. It can also throw much light on the good intent or experience of the franchisor. A great many questions need to be asked about it by the intending franchisee and his advisers in order to put the provisions of the contract into context.

There are four areas, aspects of which may not be fully covered in the contract but which require close investigation and scrutiny.

1. The product or service offered.
2. The territory and the site.
3. The relationship between the franchisee and the franchisor.
4. The nature of the franchise package.

---

* Pyramid selling is a concept in which franchisees are recruited to sell 'distributorships' while the actual product or service being distributed plays a secondary part and may, indeed, be quite unviable.

THE PRODUCT OR SERVICE

It may be new or it may be already established. There is nothing wrong with a product or service being new, provided it has been tested and found to work, preferably for at least a couple of years in a location or community similar to that for which it is now being offered (as is a condition for membership of the British Franchise Association) and provided also that the franchisee is satisfied that it enjoys a good reputation among users and customers. It is also important, of course, that the franchisee is doing something that he wants to be associated with.

Equally, there is no automatic guarantee of success in dealing with an established product or service. The franchisee must check whether the market is growing, static or declining.

Where the franchise relates to a new or established product or service, the franchisee needs to be satisfied that it has staying power (remember skateboards, the craze that was going to be with us for ever?), to what extent the demand is seasonal (people in the UK are less addicted to ice cream in winter than in some other countries) and whether its appeal is to any extent confined to a specific age group or sector of the community.

It should have some unique feature like, for instance, the 'secret recipe' of the sauce for Kentucky Fried Chicken and preferably this should be protected by a patent or trade mark.

If its success is tied to a celebrity name, the franchisee will have to find out how active the celebrity is in promoting it and judge how durable his fame is likely to be.

How competitive is the product or service in price and quality with similar ones on the market and, in particular, available in the franchisee's vicinity?

All these points were painfully brought home by the well-publicised failure in 1986 of one or two franchisors who were thought, even by the banks, to be soundly based. In each case, though, questions addressed to the actual franchisees would have shown that all was far from well. In other words, there is no substitute for first-hand investigation and research – not even expert hearsay.

The market and product (service) relationship

You must be able to satisfy yourself that the franchisor both understands and intends to preserve the essence of his strategic product/market relationship in the face of existing and likely competition. These questions will help you to probe this area.

Checklist:

☐ What is the overall demand for this type of product (or service) and what is the franchisor's market share?

☐ Is that demand seasonal? (This will affect cash flow projections and the best starting date.)

☐ Exactly what sort of people (or businesses) buy their product (or service)?

☐ What benefits do the customers get from buying the product?

☐ Who are your competitors (not just other franchisors)?

☐ What are their major strengths and weaknesses?

☐ What are your franchisor's relative advantages over that competition and why do people buy from him?

☐ How does your franchisor's quality compare?

☐ How long has this product been on the UK market?

☐ Is the product (or its image) protected by patents, copyright or trade marks?

☐ What guarantees does the product carry and who is responsible for any costs or work associated with any claims or repairs?

☐ Are there any legal or statutory controls related to the sale of this product, and if so, what are they?

☐ Are the franchisees restricted to buying stock from the franchisor?

☐ If so, how can the franchisor guarantee competitive supplies?

☐ Are franchisees allowed to extend or enhance the product range from sources other than the franchisor?

☐ How is the product advertised and promoted, and who controls and pays for that (at both national and local levels)?

☐ Are the opening hours recommended or controlled?

☐ Does the franchisor organise national sales conferences and have a 'house' sales magazine?

☐ Who sets the selling price of the product?

THE TERRITORY

Though the franchisor should provide a map showing the exact extent of the territory, this is not in itself a guarantee of absolute protection. For one thing, under EC competition laws the franchisor cannot prevent one franchisee trading in another's 'exclusive' territory, though he may decline to *license* a competitor within it; for instance, there is nothing to stop a print shop in one territory serving customers from the territory of another franchisee. There is very little that can be done about this except to check where the nearest operator of the same franchise is located or planned to be located – and indeed where operators of franchises and other businesses offering a similar product or service are to be found. The franchisee should also check whether the agreement specifies any circumstances under which his territory could be reduced.

The rationale behind the territory assignment needs to be examined. Has the franchisor picked it out arbitrarily or has he conducted – as he should have done – market surveys to indicate that the franchise is likely to be viable in that territory? These should cover aspects like traffic flows, access, population mix by age and class, and so forth, and they should be made available to the franchisee.

THE SITE

Narrowing the focus further, the franchisee should ask the same questions about the site itself. Expert advice on site selection is described as being one of the principal advantages business format franchising has to offer, but the franchisee should not allow himself to be 'blinded with science'. If he or his adviser has good reason to believe, in the light of personal knowledge of local conditions, that the site is a poor choice, then the franchisor must be pressed very hard to justify it and to demonstrate that it has the necessary qualities of visibility and accessibility to cars and pedestrians, and adequate frontage.

Access

How important each of these factors is obviously depends on what is being franchised. A take-away restaurant, for instance, would need to be accessible to both cars and pedestrians. Accessibility to cars would be less important for an ice cream parlour but vital for a product franchise where customers might need to load up their purchases.

Tenure

The method of tenure of the premises is important. Either the franchisor or the franchisee can be in the 'driving seat'. Where the franchisor holds the freehold or the lease this does not in any way remove the franchisee's security as a tenant or a licensee during the term of the agreement, but when it comes to an end his situation is less favourable. As stated earlier it is becoming more common in franchises that are operated from business premises, especially on good commercial sites, for the lease to be controlled by the franchisor.

There are grounds on which the franchisor can reclaim the premises which have nothing to do with whether the franchise was conducted satisfactorily – in particular when the franchisor is also the landlord and wants to take over the premises himself. The franchisee is then entitled to be compensated for improvements he has made to the premises, though that provision is not without potential complications:

☐ Movable fixtures and fittings are not counted as improvements. The franchisee will have to dispose of them as best he can, unless he can persuade the franchisor to buy them back or some other franchisee to take them over.

☐ The franchise contract may require a continuous scheme of improvements in order to keep the place up to standard. How the franchisee is to be compensated for such work on termination of the agreement should be spelt out in it.

☐ Check whether the rent is reasonable in relation to the neighbourhood. The difference between a lease and a licence is largely technical, except that in the case of a licence, the licensor is responsible for paying the uniform business rates.

☐ Where the lease or licence is negotiated separately from the franchise agreement, it is obviously important to check that they both cover the same time span.

Ownership of the lease or freehold confers some clear benefits. In the case of the franchisor these are that ownership creates an asset for borrowing purposes and also makes it possible for him to terminate a franchise without losing a valuable site. From the point of view of the franchisee, it makes it possible for him to divert a good site to another purpose (should he not wish to carry on with the franchise), or derive an unambiguous benefit from the sale of the site if its value has improved due either to the franchisee's efforts or to planning changes.

The territory, location or site on offer

Checklist:

☐ Is the territory exclusive, and if so, how is that exclusivity guaranteed?

☐ Who chooses the location or territory, and exactly what criteria are used to establish its commercial viability?

☐ If the franchisor makes these decisions, what will he do for you if he gets it wrong and you can't make it pay?

☐ Where are the neighbouring franchisees and company owned outlets, both current and projected?

☐ Where are the competitors?

☐ How well are other businesses doing in the area, and what are industrial and employment conditions like?

☐ Does the area present any particular insurance problems?

☐ Are any significant planning developments or road alterations expected?

☐ Is the location to be bought or leased?

☐ Are the equipment and fixtures specified by the franchisor?

☐ Do these have to be obtained from him?

☐ Is the layout of the location specified, and if so, can you make changes in the light of experience?

THE FRANCHISEE AND FRANCHISOR RELATIONSHIP

The most important questions to put to the franchisor are:

☐ how long has he been in business in the UK;
☐ how many outlets has he established in that time;
☐ how successful have they been (and what are the criteria for success)*;
☐ how many have been closed down, and for what reasons.

Failing a track record in the UK, the questions must be related to his operations elsewhere – in the USA or Europe, most probably. It would also be useful to know who the directors are and something of their qualifications, background, experience and nationality.

Foreign franchises

In the case of foreign-based franchises it is at least desirable that there should be a UK master licensee of proven status and experience. The cultural differences between consumer habits and trading customs are still powerful and foreign franchises generally need to be filtered through a process of adaptation before they are launched in another country. It is also on the cards that a franchisor's domestic market would take precedence if there was a problem over matters like supplies, unless there was a strong master licensee who could put pressure on headquarters staff.

Supplies

The success of the franchise, in terms of both profits and turnover, will be closely related to sources and costs of equipment, goods and services. These will be controlled, wholly or in part, by the franchisor. The franchisee needs to be sure that the prices are fair and competitive and that supply is likely to be trouble-free. There

---

* Financial information should be checked by an accountant.

might, for instance, be question marks where goods have to be obtained from Third World countries with political problems. Some franchisors set a minimum ordering quantity for supplies and this has to be realistic in relation to the franchisee's resources and his expectations in terms of business volume. Ideally, though, the franchisee should not be too closely tied to the franchisor or the nominees as a main source since this obviously gives the franchisor a degree of leverage which is open to abuse. Indeed, some good franchise agreements leave franchisees the option to buy elsewhere if goods from sources suggested or even nominated by the franchisor are uncompetitive or unobtainable.

Standards of quality

Quality management is starting to appeal to franchisors. At least one franchisor, Kall-Kwik, has embarked on a programme to help its franchisees attain BS 5750.

The franchisee should establish such aspects of the relationship as:

☐ what standards of quality are being set (and the cost implications of this);
☐ what opening hours have to be kept (again these may have implications in terms of staffing and overtime payments); and
☐ what the reporting procedures are for accounting purposes.

Even though the franchisee is running his own business, the franchisor will want to check that royalties being paid accurately reflect the volume of business and he will also demand the right to enter and inspect the premises at will.

Future developments

The business format is not a constant. It may be amended from time to time and the franchisee will have to go along with the amendments. Therefore it is important to establish, as far as possible, what the franchisor's future plans are:

☐ Has he got any costly innovations up his sleeve?

☐   Is he planning any new franchises or other moves that may be in competition with the franchises he is now offering?

☐   Is he doing things which might stretch the financial and human resources of his existing operation to its detriment?

In all of these cases, the franchisee might suffer.

Termination

The conditions under which the franchise can be terminated by either party, assigned or renewed should be clearly spelt out. There should be a satisfactory disputes procedure. Arbitration in such cases has become a popular alternative to litigation since the 1979 Arbitration Act, and the BFA is encouraging its use as a standard dispute practice by its members. It is also campaigning for its extension to non-members, who can refer to the BFA in such circumstances.

Checklist:

☐   Is the franchisor soundly financed? Ask to see the recently audited financial statements, and look at least three years back too.

☐   Is the franchisor a subsidiary of another company and if so whom?

☐   Is that parent company soundly financed? Ask to see their audited accounts too.

☐   Does the franchisor have associate companies? If so, who are they and what exactly is their relationship?

☐   Does either the parent company or any associate operate franchises?

☐   If they do, would they be in competition with you?

☐   Is their franchise operation(s) a success?

☐   How long has the franchisor been in this type of business?

☐   When did he start franchising?

☐   How long has his pilot operation(s) been running?

☐   Does he maintain an outlet as a testing ground for new ideas and product improvements?

☐   Does the franchisor still run any outlets himself, and if so, how many?

☐ Are they buy-backs of failed franchisees or does he tend to keep prime sites for himself?

☐ What business experience and qualifications have the franchisor's directors and managers, and what is the structure of their organisation?

☐ How much of their own cash do the directors have in the business?

☐ Have any of the directors or managers ever gone bankrupt?

☐ Have they or the company recently been involved in litigation, county court judgments etc?

☐ What is the franchisor's commercial credit rating?

☐ How many franchise outlets does the franchisor currently have in the UK, and what has been the trend over the past three to five years?

☐ Has he had any franchise failures or departures? If so, how many, and when and why did they fail?

☐ How many franchisee and owner-operated outlets does he plan to have in future and over what time scale? Where will they be?

☐ Can you interview a selection of the franchisees of your own choice? Choose a mixture of experienced and new franchisees in different types of location.

☐ Who are the franchisor's accountants, bankers, lawyers, and are there any other professional or commercial references that you can take up?

☐ What selection criteria are used for choosing franchisees? How many are turned away?

☐ What innovations has the franchisor introduced since he started franchising, and what plans does he have for the future (new products, services, markets etc)?

☐ Is the franchisor a member of the BFA or any other appropriate trade body or chamber of commerce?

☐ If it is a foreign company, how many of the answers to the above questions relate to their UK operations?

THE FRANCHISE PACKAGE

To a large extent the package determines and overlaps the nature of the franchisor/franchisee relationship, but it has characteristics of its own. Fees are most important here: not only how much, but the form in which they are paid. There will be an initial fee, a royalty on turnover and/or a mark-up on goods supplied for resale, but there can be considerable – and significant – differences in the amounts and the way they are collected. In general, the advice is to be very careful about franchises with a high initial fee and a low royalty (unless, of course, the franchisor receives part of his income in the form of a mark-up on goods supplied): the franchisor may be of the 'take your money and run' variety. Equally, low royalties may reflect a high mark-up on the tied supply of goods and services. The question then is whether the product being offered is competitive in price. A low initial fee is not necessarily favourable either – it may mask high royalties or hidden charges.

Another point to watch out for is whether the franchisor sets a minimum figure the franchisee must pay, irrespective of income from the franchise. If so, is the amount reasonable? Here again, the advice of an accountant would be invaluable.

Advertising

Related to the question of fees is that of advertising. Increasingly this is being shown as a separate and additional charge, currently an average of 2.6 per cent of turnover. The question then is whether it is dedicated to the franchise as a whole or to promoting individual outlets. In both cases the franchisee needs to be satisfied that the advertising is good and relevant, both as regards content and medium. This question should also be asked where the franchisor imposes a specific advertising levy, separate from the royalty – a growing practice.

Local press, radio, TV and cinema advertising is most helpful to the franchisee. National campaigns are costly and the purpose behind them may be to sell franchises rather than to further the franchisee's particular business. Nevertheless, some national advertising may be essential if a nationwide franchise chain is to be developed, with its knock-on benefits to individual franchisees. In the USA, for example, McDonald's, one of the world's largest franchisors, spends more on TV advertising than Kelloggs, and virtually the same as the Ford Motor Company.

Point of sale, counter and window advertising is also important in this latter respect and the agreement should state who pays for it. If the franchisor requires such advertising to be done, then it could represent a sizeable additional cost to the franchisee.

Training

Another area where who pays for what needs to be clarified is that of training. Indeed, since training is in itself a very important part of the package, the franchisee must know how much there will be and how long it will take. In America the concept of training is sometimes taken to ludicrous lengths – McDonald's operate a Hamburger University and one suspects it is only partly meant as a joke, if at all. However, training should cover such basic skills as operating methods, financial controls, and the care and maintenance of equipment, as well as instruction on how to carry out the various statutory requirements – employment legislation, calculating PAYE, VAT, and so forth – with which the owner of a business is expected to comply.

There is also the question of refresher courses, employee training and instruction in new methods. In each case the franchisee should be clear as to what extent training is compulsory or necessary, whether it is the subject of extra charges and how these are arrived at. Chapter 7 will look more closely at this issue.

Apart from formal training and refresher courses, there ought also to be some procedure for when things go wrong. What happens if the franchisee falls ill? Can an emergency crew step in? And what happens if the franchisee runs into administrative or equipment trouble? Is help of sufficient calibre available, how quickly and at what cost?

Operating manual

The operating manual embodies the 'blueprint' of the business format franchise and some contracts state that its status is paramount over anything that is said in the agreement. The franchisee and his advisers must be sure that they fully understand the manual and that it covers all the situations they are likely to encounter in operating the franchise. It is also worth finding out how often it is updated and when the last update took place.

While many of these points will be covered in the contract or provided as general background by the franchisor, there are two important aspects which the franchisee will have to evaluate but which will not be part of the standard information package: what is known about the franchisor himself and the experience of other franchisees.

Fees

The 1998 NatWest/BFA survey points to what seems to be a trend to 'lower entry costs, but then to seek more of a contribution once the franchise is established'. The average total initial outlay for setting up a franchise is £43,700, slightly lower than a year ago, while the average service fee has remained at 10 per cent of turnover. Such averages, though, mask some quite considerable variations between franchises, which relate to the kind of business being conducted, taken from the survey.

A variation not listed occurs in the case of the management services fee where the franchisee buys the product he sells from the franchisor. In that case the franchisor derives his profits mainly from that activity, and should not be charging much more than 5 to 6 per cent of turnover by way of a management fee.

The advertising charge of around 4.2 per cent of turnover is fairly uniform for all types of franchise. However, franchisees should be satisfied that the charge is indeed being applied to promoting the franchised activity to customers, not merely to recruiting franchisees.

The franchise package and after-sales service and support

Checklist:

☐ Does the franchisor provide an initial business and product training programme for you?

- ☐ If so, how long, what exactly is the content and who pays for it?
- ☐ Does the franchisor provide pre-launch advertising and promotions?
- ☐ Will the franchisor provide a launch team to help you open up, and if so, who pays?
- ☐ Does the franchisor help select and train your staff? Are there any restrictions on whom you can employ?
- ☐ Does the franchisor provide an operating manual that explains all aspects of running the business?
- ☐ Who pays for the initial opening supplies?
- ☐ What provision does the franchisor make for counselling and advice with operating problems? (Ask to meet the staff responsible for providing such a service.)
- ☐ Does the franchisor provide regular post-opening training, if necessary?
- ☐ Is there a system for inspecting a franchisee's business operations?
- ☐ How is quality control monitored both on franchisor supplies and franchisee operations?
- ☐ What 'business systems' are provided, such as book-keeping, stock control etc?
- ☐ Can the franchisor advise on appropriate professional help – accountants, surveyors, lawyers etc?
- ☐ Is an initial supply of business stationery etc included in the package?
- ☐ Can the franchisor prove that his support systems really work?

THE FRANCHISOR

A good franchisor will ask the franchisee a lot of questions (often by way of a questionnaire sent with a response to an initial enquiry) about his qualifications to run a business: about experience, health, financial resources and so forth. Indeed, to some extent the more searching such questions are the better, because it indicates that the franchisor has a close interest in the good and successful conduct of each outlet. The current shortage of suitable franchisees has led franchisors to be more specific about the skills and experience that they are looking for. Chapter 6 examines this subject in greater depth. Equally, though, the franchisee should be ready with some questions of his own.

Apart from those that come under the heading of franchisor/franchisee relationship, it is important to establish the following:

☐ When was the company started?
☐ How long was it in operation with the product or services before it started franchising it? (It takes at least two or three years for a franchisor to get the bugs out of the system.)
☐ Is the franchisor a member of the BFA, which is conditional on proper piloting? If not it is essential that the scheme should have bank support.
☐ What plans are there for future growth? Rapid expansion could cause administrative problems and established retailing and fast food franchises have often adopted a policy of expanding only along viable lines of supply.
☐ Ask your bank manager or accountant to check on the franchisor's financial standing.
☐ Find out whether the business history of the principals is related to the product or service they are franchising. They may merely have bought into an established company without having experience of running a franchise.
☐ Find out the size of the headquarters' staff and whether or not they work full time. You could also visit the franchisor's premises and form your own judgement about its appearance and the quality of staff.
☐ Find out if the franchisor is operating any outlets himself as he may be keeping the best to himself or re-purchasing the less successful ones in order to preserve a respectable track record.

THE EXPERIENCES OF OTHER FRANCHISEES

The most reliable proof of the pudding is in its eating and you should certainly talk to other franchisees before committing yourself. They should be those who have been in business for at least a couple of years and the outlet they are operating should be similar to the one you are contemplating in terms of size and catchment area. The following questions need to be asked:

Checklist:

☐ What total investment was required; not only the down payment to the franchisor, but additional costs in the way of equipment etc?

☐ Were the franchisor's projections of costs and revenues reasonably accurate?

☐ Did the franchisors live up to their promises regarding help with launching the business, training, promotional back-up?

☐ Was the operating manual practical and easy to follow?

☐ Is the product good enough? Are service and deliveries to the franchisee prompt and efficient?

☐ When problems arise, how long does it take for troubleshooters or the franchisor's repair men or other services provided by the franchisor to materialise?

☐ What disagreements have arisen with the franchisor, over what? Were they settled satisfactorily?

☐ What proof does the franchisor require of turnover and profitability? Are they reasonable and easy to comply with?

☐ How much inspection does the franchisor impose on the conduct of the franchise? Is it reasonable?

☐ What unexpected expenses have been incurred and for what reason?

☐ How long did it take the business to reach break-even, including paying the franchisee the level of income he expected to get and a return on his investment?

☐ If you could change anything in the contract with the wisdom of hindsight, what would it be?

☐ Does the product have a steady and continuing sale or is it subject to seasonal, or even weekly or daily, peaks and troughs?

This sort of information is best gleaned from a franchisee in whom you have no personal interest – in other words not from one whose franchise you are thinking of taking over, because he will tell you only the good things, not the bad ones. It is also important to talk to more than one franchisee, and not all of them should be names given to you by the franchisor. Equally, though, if the franchisor shows any reluctance over letting you talk to other franchisees, it could be taken as a bad sign. However, if you put together all the methods of evaluating a franchise shown in this chapter, it should enable you and your advisers to check whether the franchise bears out the franchisor's claims about its performance.

4 Financial Viability

Presumably you are taking out a franchise in the hope of making money, or at least a reasonable living, in a way that is congenial to you. Chapter 5 deals with the personal factors; here we look at the financial aspects, and ask the question: When you are presented with a set of figures by your franchisor, what should you be looking for? This process is known as *interpretation of accounts* and breaks down into two areas:

1. How healthy is the franchisor's organisation as a whole?
2. How attractive is the particular franchise opportunity that you are being offered?

Some of the answers to the first question are provided in Chapter 11, but you may not actually start talking to a franchisor until some months after you read this book, and in the meantime he may have filed another set of annual accounts which you will need to inspect to see whether the trends are healthy.

INTERPRETING THE FRANCHISOR'S ACCOUNTS

The first step is to find out whether the franchisor is operating as a limited company, and if so what its name is; it may not be the same as the trading name. For example, Kall-Kwik Printing is the trading name of KK Printing (UK) Limited. If the company will not give you a set of its audited accounts and you would like

,more information than is provided here or by the most recent accounts, you will need to get it from Companies House. Most of the larger franchises are limited companies; a few of the smaller and newer ones are sole traders or partnerships, in which case their accounts are not publicly available. However, you should still try to see them before you commit yourself to the franchise.

When you get your copy of the accounts you will find that there are two financial documents, the _profit and loss account_ and the _balance sheet_, and a number of legal forms and records.

The profit and loss account

- [ ] The profit and loss account shows the income generated and expenditure incurred by the company.
- [ ] The balance sheet shows the picture of a business at a particular moment in time. It shows where a business has got its money from and what it has done with that money.

An understanding of financial reports is essential to anyone who wants to invest in acquiring and running a business. To be effective, the businessman must be able to analyse and interpret that financial information.

All analysis of financial information requires comparisons and there are three yardsticks against which business performance can be measured:

- [ ] How well a franchisor is meeting a personal goal by comparing actual results with his budget.
- [ ] Comparing current performance with previous years measures growth in sales and profits.
- [ ] How well the franchisor is doing compared with competitors or with someone in a similar line of business. Will identify where improvement can be made. Information can be found in Companies House and in trade directories.

What results are you looking for?

You should be looking for financial results in two areas that are vital to a business's chances of survival:

☐ *Satisfactory level of profit.* The business has to give a satisfactory return to shareholders – or the owner(s) – bearing in mind the risk they are taking, and this should match building society rates. A business must also make enough profit if it is to grow.

☐ *Survival.* To survive, the business must be financially sound. You should be concerned about high financial risks including running out of cash, or of the franchises being so heavily borrowed that the interest charges weigh the business down.

How sound is the financial position?

Maintaining a sound financial position for most businesses seems to be focused on keeping away from overgearing or overtrading, the two rocks on which many founder. You have to be confident the franchisor is going to be around for long enough to deliver his end of the contract!

☐ *Overgearing.* This is when a business has a high proportion of outside money to inside money. For a new business with no substantial historical profits to invest in future growth, borrowing money represents the only option. However, research into reasons for the failure of companies given loans under the government loan guarantee scheme shows that a start-up gearing greater than 4:1 is nearly always fatal. You should also identify the business's capacity to pay interest.

☐ *Overtrading.* A term used to describe a business which is expanding beyond its capacity to get additional working capital resources. As sales expand, the money tied up in stocks and customers' credit grows rapidly. The answer to this is an overdraft. However, many businesses do not recognise the dangers in time.

How attractive is the proposition you are considering?

At the very minimum you will expect the franchisor to give you a breakdown of the capital you will be expected to provide, and what it will be used to buy, and a projected profit and loss account, perhaps showing different results according to the level of sales achieved.

The example below is for Gamesters Ltd, a hypothetical games shop franchise. You can see that two projections have been put forward, one for annual sales of £104,000 which the franchisor might propose as a 'worst scenario'. The other for £156,000 is perhaps seen as the most likely outcome. If you, the franchisee,

Gamesters Ltd

Capital outlay:	£			
Shop fittings	24,000			
Equipment	8,000			
Stock	20,000			
Franchise fee	6,000			
Sundries	2,000			
	60,000			

Profit forecast	1		2	
Sales	104,000		156,000	
Less cost of sales	46,800		70,200	
Gross margin		57,200		85,800
Less expenses:				
Franchise royalty (5%)	5,200		7,800	
Advertising fund (2%)	2,000		3,000	
Wages, NI	22,000		33,000	
Rent, rates, insurance	10,000		15,000	
Heat, light, power	1,000		1,500	
Postage and telephone	800		1,200	
Motor and travel	1,400		2,100	
Accountancies and professional services	1,200		1,800	
Depreciation	3,000	46,600	3,000	68,400
Profit		10,600		17,400

proposed to work in the business then no doubt a large chunk of the wages element of expense could also be viewed as your 'profit'. Although not shown here, it would not be unusual for a third projection to be presented, showing a 'best case' scenario. Just as the worst scenario is supposed to represent a position the franchisor could not envisage in his worst nightmare, the best case is often put forward as what you could achieve, 'if you really pull out all the stops'.

It is, however, probably unfair to judge franchisors solely on the basis of information included in their publicity brochures; the franchisors have their business to protect and as they are dealing with individuals who have at least some entrepreneurial spirit, there is a risk of their costings being used by someone else to set up independently. This possibility cannot be eliminated, so anyone who is being asked to part with a fee should demand a detailed breakdown first, but it need not be made too available to the general public.

Assuming that the franchisor has got the start-up costs right, in many cases he is in a position to put the franchisee in touch with sources of finance. If the franchisor has made arrangements with a bank for the provision of loans then there is some reassurance that the proposition has been examined and approved (or at least not rejected) by someone with some experience: an important point when the franchisor is not one of the old established or household names.

It is important to have a clear idea of the start-up costs and capital requirements of a franchise, if only because these are going to be a prime determinant of the franchise chosen.

Leasing

Leasing is another method of avoiding high initial capital expenditure, but at the cost of raising the overhead running costs and a certain loss of flexibility – leased assets cannot be used as security, nor can they be sold. It may not be possible to terminate the agreement without substantial penalties being incurred, which could be a disadvantage should the equipment be found to be unsuitable, or inferior to another available product.

Anticipated profitability

This has to be the crucial area for examination. The potential franchisee wants to make, if not a fortune, at least a living. The downside of the increased security and reduction of risk that are the attractions of franchising also mean that the potential rewards are likely to be lower.

Various estimates in the industry indicate that it takes an average of 2.4 years for a franchisee to break even on initial investment. To keep things simple these figures do not allow for taxation on profits but, of course, depending on personal circumstances, tax may be due.

Looking at an actual forecast, again taking Gamesters Ltd as our example: John Smith, a hypothetical person, having some experience in selling and repairing computer games, considered taking out a Gamester franchise, but eventually decided to go it alone. However, he found the predicted costings he had been given useful, and prepared his business plan on the basis of them. He obtained finance from the bank under the loan guarantee scheme. Now, after about 18 months' trading, he is in severe financial difficulties because of cash flow problems, and the business could fail in the next few months.

Doubtless Gamesters would say that this merely proves that he should have had the strength of the franchise company behind him, but it is instructive to see where his costs differed from those predicted.

First, the cost of sales figure was too low. Recent increases in the cost of computer boards and other materials meant that 50 per cent was consumed in this way, rather than the 45 per cent projected, so reducing profits by £7280. The rent, rates and insurance figure was underestimated by £3000 (the figure might have been adequate in a less populous neighbourhood).

Capital costs, too, were higher than expected. Shopfitting came to £30,000 and increases in equipment costs added a further £2000. This extra £8000 led to a 13 per cent increase in depreciation to £3390.

If Gamester's figures are adjusted for these amounts, the profit of £10,600 in their 'worst case' reduces to a loss of £70 (£7280 + £3000 + £390).

This example shows how easily a franchisor's projected profit can be turned into an actual loss. It is absolutely vital to test every figure in the franchisor's projection, by probing questions and personal research. Then re-cast the figures yourself, challenging the franchisor to prove his case. This must all be done before the contract is signed.

TAKING OVER AN EXISTING FRANCHISE OUTLET

Whether you are considering taking over an existing franchise outlet, or a new one, many of the points you should consider are exactly the same. However, the existence of another party, the vendor, introduces some complications but makes certain problems less worrying.

If there is an existing outlet for sale, then you have the reassurance that the franchise organisation has some proven value; you do not have to take the same risks as with a new franchise, where all you may be able to rely on is the franchisor's pilot operation. All the same, all the questions that arise as to the viability of the franchisor's organisation and the terms of the franchise contract should still be considered just as carefully.

The main difference from taking up a new outlet is the availability of more information. Instead of the franchisor presenting you with a set of 'typical' start-up costs and a projected profit and loss account for a 'typical' unit, there will be a definite cost, the purchase price, and definite accounts.

The first point that you should ascertain is why the vendors are selling. No one willingly sells the proverbial 'little gold mine'. You do not want to purchase a business which is being sold because the owners cannot make a living out of it, unless you have good reason to think that you could do better. This may, in fact, be the case. For example, someone might take out a franchise of a 24-hour plumbing or drain clearing service after being made redundant from a nine-to-five office job and discover, after trying to adjust for a year or so, that he simply cannot cope with the type of work, or the erratic hours, and decide to get out. He has made a mistake as to the type of business he should have been in, but that does not mean there is necessarily anything wrong with the franchise itself, as long as you are convinced that you will not make the same mistake.

Where the reasons for sale are given as being personal, you should try to check up on the facts. The death of the proprietor is probably the most convincing personal reason; explanations such as illness, wish to move to be nearer relatives etc should be viewed, not necessarily with scepticism, but certainly as possibly not being the whole truth. If there are employees, a talk to them may help verify the reasons given.

Assuming that the franchise outlet has been in existence for some time, you should expect to be given at least three years' accounts. Once you start to go back beyond three years, then the information becomes rather of academic interest, given changing conditions. You now have to decide how much reliance to place on the accounts you are given. At this point consultation with an accountant will probably be advisable. If the vendors were operating as a limited company, then you should demand to see the audited accounts; but as these disclose only minimum information (they do not, for example, require so necessary a figure as the gross margin to be disclosed), you will also require the detailed accounts that the management uses.

If the vendor was a sole trader or a partnership then there will not be 'audited' accounts. There will, however, be accounts prepared for the proprietors, if only in order to agree the tax liability with the Inland Revenue. Here you should be quite clear about the function of the accountant. Except when he is auditing the statutory accounts of a limited company, when his duties are laid down by law, he is acting for his client and on his instructions. Most accounts prepared for sole traders and partnerships have a qualification such as 'These accounts were prepared from books and records presented to us, and information given to us by the client, and are in accordance therewith. We have not carried out an audit.' In other words, if the vendor has misled the accountant the accounts will be wrong, and the accountant will accept no responsibility.

You should make a distinction between the possibility that the accounts are definitely misleading or even fraudulent, and the probability that they will show a somewhat pessimistic view. As stated above, most sole trader and partnership year-end accounts are prepared for presentation to the Inland Revenue, and there is therefore a tendency to depress the profit figures in order to minimise the tax liability. You should not, however, accept from the vendor a grossly different figure based on this fact. If his accountant holds a reputable qualification there are requirements of professional ethics from his professional body that mean there are limits on how far he can deviate from what he knows to be the case; he certainly cannot falsify information, though there is some latitude in obscuring it. If the accountant is unqualified, these restraints do not necessarily apply, but even so, no accountant who has a regard for his professional reputation is likely to be willing to endanger it for one client.

Assuming that you have decided the accounts are reliable, you should also consider additional information such as:

☐ A trend to increasing profits; certainly a turnover figure and a profit figure which increase at least greater than inflation. When looking at the profit figure you should see whether any amounts have been taken out by way of management salary by the vendors, as what you are interested in is the total profit available to you.

☐ A comparison of the figures with the franchisor's 'typical' figures. Investigate any material differences.

☐ How your own costs might differ; for example, if you intended to employ more people your wage costs would rise.

☐ The employees who you will be taking over; under the Employment Regulations any terms and conditions of employment that were agreed by employees with the previous owner of the business are also binding on the new one. That may stop you, for instance, paying anyone less than they were getting before.

☐ The vendor probably wants to sell to you at least as much as you want to buy from him; unlike the deal with the franchisor, there is likely to be considerable leeway for negotiation on the price he is asking.

This could also be true where an already established business is turning branches into franchised outlets – a practice which many observers think is likely to grow. However, skilled professional advice on the accounts and a good deal of research into the viability of the site are essential – plus your own personal judgement of the situation. Why is such a switch being made? You have to be realistic about the fact that a franchisor of this kind is unlikely to franchise his most profitable branches. If the trade is not there, franchising is unlikely to change the situation. The potential for achieving good profits by cutting costs and better management must be evident.

Occasionally, an established business, having made the decision to grow via the franchising route, will sell off some or all of its existing outlets. An example is Holland & Barrett, when they had 150 company-owned outlets but their market research indicated that the UK could support around 2,000 health food shops a decade later. To maintain their 20 per cent share of this market they would need a further 300 or so outlets. With three manufacturing subsidiaries to finance in this rapidly expanding market, Holland & Barrett opted for franchising as a way forward in the retail market. As a consequence a number of 'quality' outlets were put on to the market.

When considering buying an existing outlet a prospective buyer should question the parent company's management closely on their strategy, and on their commitment to franchising. Holland & Barrett's boss, Ken Mullarkey, stated at the time that, 'there are some clear reasons why our form of retailing lends itself more to franchising than some others. There is a strong element of personal service – it isn't a supermarket operation. People come in asking for advice on what products they should buy to achieve a particular aim – like healthy ways of losing weight for instance.'

However, there is a lesson in the Holland & Barrett story. Though there was no doubt about the quality of their product, it turned out that health foods are not accepted in equal measure throughout the country. They did well in middle class neighbourhoods in the South-East, less well elsewhere. The socio-economic character of the market which a franchise is serving is an important consideration in evaluating it as a business proposition.

PERFORMANCE SUMMARY

In the final analysis the measure of success in franchising is: do the franchisees make money? The latest figures from the NatWest and the BFA present a mixed picture here. They show that 8 per cent are loss-making, slightly down on last year's percentage; 56 per cent are 'highly profitable' or 'quite profitable', but the remaining 36 per cent are 'marginally profitable'. However, a further breakdown of the results indicates that franchises' profit performance over time improves slightly.

Franchisee claimed unit profitability

	All franchisees			Time franchise held		
	1995	1996	1997	Up to 2 years	3–4 years	5 years plus
	%	%	%	%	%	%
Highly profitable	5	11	3	5	1	4
Quite profitable	37	47	53	36	41	67
Marginally profitable	48	36	36	40	49	28
	(90)	(94)	(92)	(81)	(91)	(99)
Just loss making	6	4	5	12	9	1
Definitely loss making	4	2	3	7	–	–
	(10)	(6)	(8)	(19)	(9)	(1)

These results show an encouraging pattern of profitable trading. On the other hand, there are some factors which give rise to caution. The number of franchisees reporting 'highly profitable' results has slightly declined in the past year. And even after holding a franchise for more than five years, only 4 per cent of franchisees claim to be highly profitable. Over the first four years around 10 per cent of franchisees are still reporting losses.

Franchise start-up costs, operating costs, projected revenues and profits

Checklist:

☐ How much does the licence fee cost and what exactly do you get for it?

☐ Is there any initial deposit, and if so, is it returnable in full?

☐ How much long-term capital will you need to buy leases, equipment, fixtures etc?

☐ How much working capital will you need to finance stock, debtors etc?

☐ Do you have to buy certain minimum quantities of stock and other supplies from the franchisor, and if so, what happens if your sales are too low?

☐ How much will the franchise package cost you, and what does it consist of?

☐ What are the royalty charges throughout the life of this agreement?

☐ Are there any provisions for altering the royalty level when sales are poor – ie below break-even volume?

☐ Are goods supplied by the franchisor marked up? If so, by how much?

☐ Is there any control on increases in mark-up?

☐ Do you have to make a regular commitment to 'central' advertising? If so, how much and how often?

☐ How often will you have to replace equipment, machinery etc? Do you have a choice of both time and type?

☐ How often will you have to redecorate?

☐ What financing arrangements can the franchisor make for you? What are the terms and conditions associated with this finance, ie true interest rate, loan repayment period, capital moratoriums etc? Will you end up owning the equipment after all financing costs have been paid off?

☐ What does the franchisor expect sales revenue to be month by month for the first 12 months and quarterly for the next two years?

☐ What does the franchisor expect material and operating costs to be (on the same basis as above)?

☐ So what will the projected gross and net profits be over the first three years? (Make sure your salary and interest on loans and overdrafts are deducted.)

☐ How can the franchisor substantiate these projections? If based on other franchisees' experiences, can you see audited results? (Take a copy for your accountant to examine.)

☐ What legal or other contractual fees are likely to be incurred in taking out this franchise?

☐ Are there any other costs or revenues associated with running this franchise?

5 | Evaluating Yourself

SUITABILITY FOR SELF-EMPLOYMENT

No less important than evaluating the franchise, and the organisation behind it, is the question of evaluating your own suitability for self-employment. This is not just a question of financial resources, nor is a desire for independence, however passionately felt, enough in itself. Even a willingness to work hard, important though that is as a first step, is no more than one of several qualities you will need to make a success of setting up in business on your own. In fact, one of the problems of self-employment is that few people realise just how much work is involved. They may pride themselves on never having been clock watchers as employees of someone else, but that usually meant working long hours when they were called on to do so – once or twice a month perhaps, or even a couple of times a week. To a self-employed person long hours are normal, and the 'normal' working day of others the exception.

One reason for this is that working for yourself is not just a matter of doing the one job. People launching out on their own after years of working for others tend to forget what a warm, comfortable place the organisation is. 'Someone' looks after the PAYE and VAT returns, 'someone' does the paperwork, orders supplies, chases up goods that have failed to arrive, checks that the right instructions have been given to the right people and that they have been carried out. Maybe you will be or have been that 'someone' for one or other of these jobs as an employee, but as 'head cook and bottlewasher' in your own firm you will be that 'someone' for each and every one of these tasks. Even on days when you would have taken time off for sickness had you been employed, you will probably have to turn up to check on things, so good health is as important in self-employment as a healthy bank balance.

FAMILY SUPPORT

The healthy bank balance is not something you will achieve quickly. With the exception of a very few lucky people, most of those who have opted for self-employment report that the price of independence is a high one and that, for the hours worked, the money is worse than they were making as an employee, at least during the first two or three years. For this reason it is important to have an understanding family behind you, if you have a family at all. They may not see very much of you for a while. You will find it difficult to take holidays, and the weekends which you may previously have spent taking them out in the car or cutting the hedge, are now more likely to be devoted to poring over the accounts or making up the order book. In fact, it helps enormously if you can persuade members of your family to take part in the business. Apart from the psychological advantages of the fact that they might better understand the pressures you are under, there are tax advantages to employing your wife in the business. Assuming she has no other source of income, she is then eligible for a tax-free allowance on the first £4,195 of her earnings. These days, when so many young people are out of work, there may also be other members of the family who would be very glad of the chance of a job.

LEADERSHIP AND DISCIPLINE

This is another important aspect of self-employment in which many people have little experience. It is notoriously difficult to keep young people in order at home and it becomes no easier in a work situation – though probably considerably more important. Successful franchising depends heavily on maintaining standards of appearance, cleanliness and time-keeping. The failure to do so is taken as a breach of contract and can eventually lead to its cancellation by the franchisor. Operating a franchise means leading by example and becoming fairly tough on discipline. That does not mean standing over the staff with a whip, but it does entail a readiness to take unpopular decisions, including sacking staff if all else fails.

PERSONAL CHARACTERISTICS

Most important of all, perhaps, is that you should evaluate whether you are actually going to enjoy the work. Career consultants have come to the conclusion that no matter how you test people, whatever ways you measure aptitudes and put together lists of personal characteristics that are required for specific types of jobs, success or failure largely depends on whether they like what they are doing. In addition to checking out the franchise itself and whether it lives up to the franchisor's performance promises, it is absolutely vital that it should be something you actually want to do. If you don't like dealing with the public, or hate cooking, a fast food franchise is not for you. If the product is not something you would actually want for yourself, the franchise is probably not for you either. Quite apart from that, some personal characteristics might indicate that, although self-employment is a good idea for you, the particular form of it which franchising offers is not. Franchising does entail a good deal of uniformity in operating methods and presentation of the product, and if you are a person who does not take kindly to having his work inspected and who likes to take a very independent line, you may find yourself on a collision course before long. Perhaps the best way of discovering whether you are cut out to be a franchisee is to follow that old training officer's learning method of 'sitting next to Nellie'; in other words, having a spell working in the sort of franchise you are thinking of taking on to see whether it really suits you. Even if you do it for no pay, it could be worth hundreds of pounds in terms of experience.

A study of the personal franchisee characteristics required for success, carried out by Professor Russell M Knight of the University of Western Ontario, concluded that franchisees and franchisors had a large measure of agreement on what made for success.

They disagreed only in rating management ability and creativity – a point that may provide some clues as to what franchisors are really looking for in a franchisee.

Personal franchisee characteristics required for success

		Franchisee %			Franchisor %		
		Very important	Important	Not important	Very important	Important	Not important
☐	Previous management experience in same industry	0	20	80	2	14	84
☐	Previous own business experience	12	46	42	16	47	37
☐	Management ability	84	15	1	66	31	3
☐	Desire to succeed	90	10	0	93	7	0
☐	Willingness to work hard	92	8	0	93	6	1
☐	Creativity	26	56	18	12	44	44
☐	Strong people skills	63	32	5	64	34	2
☐	Financial backing	71	27	2	67	27	6
☐	Support from family	52	28	20	46	32	22

(Study size: 148 franchisors and 105 franchisees replied to questionnaire with follow-up interviews with 25 members of each group.)

QUESTIONNAIRE

In the meantime, here are some questions to ask yourself which have a good deal of bearing on your general suitability for self-employment as a franchisee:

☐ Do you like dealing with the general public, or are you shy and reserved?

☐ Do you work well on your own initiative, or do you find you perform better when others tell you what to do?

☐ In the sort of situations that running a business is likely to involve, do you lead or follow?

☐ Are you a good organiser and administrator?
☐ Are there some tasks which you hate doing, either because you find them boring or because you are no good at them, but which you might nevertheless be involved in when running your own business?
☐ Can you work very long hours for long periods of time or do you tire easily?
☐ Is your health good?
☐ Can you be sure of moral and maybe physical support from your family?
☐ Are you easily discouraged by setbacks or do you see things through regardless?
☐ Do you make decisions readily? Are they good ones?
☐ Can you be tough with people when you have to be?
☐ Are you good at listening to advice and even criticism, or are you touchy and impatient about it?

6 | What are Franchisors Looking For?

SUITABLE APPLICANTS

The most recent NatWest/BFA survey asked franchisors what they consider to be the biggest barrier to the growth of the number of franchised units they operate in the UK. By far the greatest number of respondents – 39 per cent – said that it was the lack of suitable franchisees that inhibited growth. This finding has led the report's authors to suggest that, 'The apparent lack of suitable franchisees is seen as the only significant growth barrier and illustrates a need for more enterprising individuals to consider franchising as an option.'

And yet, no matter how necessary it is to encourage more 'enterprising' applicants into franchising, the problem remains that should anyone be too independent or entrepreneurial it is unlikely that they will happily conform to somebody else's system. Franchising attracts large numbers of people precisely because it is considered to be less risky than starting up alone, and because it is formulaic. Franchisors look for people who are self-motivated and enterprising but are likely to have limits as to the level of franchisee independence that will be acceptable within their system. For example, Pam Bader, Chief Executive of the domestic cleaning franchisor Molly Maid, lists 'a positive approach to learning, applying and sticking to the Molly Maid system' as being among the personal qualities looked for in prospective franchisees.

Given that the interest in franchising remains strong it appears that applicants do accept these constraints in return for the backing of an established name and proven concept. Visit any franchise exhibition and the number of people interested in becoming franchisees is clear. Reputable franchisors receive many more applications from people hoping to take up a franchise than they have territories to offer. The British Franchise Association suggests that the selection of individual franchisees should be guided as follows: 'A franchisor should select and accept as individual franchisees only those who, upon reasonable investigation, appear to possess the basic skills, education, personal qualities and financial resources sufficient to carry on the franchised business.' However, while elements such as work experience do still count, the BFA's advice misses the fact that many franchisors say that it is that 'something else' that makes all the difference. That 'something else' appears to be the personal attributes and characteristics of prospective franchisees and it is identifying these that has become the main focus of franchisors' interviews in the quest for suitable applicants.

Unfortunately, these attributes tend not to be things that you can bottle and sell. Much of it relies on personal chemistry with the interviewer and being able to fit in with the company culture. However, being aware of the kind of attributes that franchisors tend to look for will help in the preparation of interviews. Just thinking about what examples can be used from former employment or life experience may well help strengthen your appeal.

PERSONAL ATTRIBUTES

Whether inherent in your personality or developed as learned skills, attributes such as self-motivation and tenacity are developed over many years and are not things that can be 'crammed' a few weeks before having an interview. The following characteristics are among those that many franchisors look for in potential franchisees:

- [ ] eagerness;
- [ ] ability to work hard;
- [ ] management ability;
- [ ] good communication and 'people' skills;

☐ family support;
☐ aspiration to succeed.

Greg Clarke's book, *Buying Your First Franchise*, suggests that before an interview it is worth carrying out a self-examination. He advises that this personal assessment should cover the following aspects:

☐ Your willingness to work hard.
☐ Your desire to succeed.
☐ Your ability to plan, implement and control the business in terms of your resources of time and money.
☐ Your likely attention to administration, the recording of financial information and your skill in managing finance.
☐ Your own personal objectives and clarity of purpose.
☐ Your temperament, attributes and abilities.
☐ Your capacity to learn and adapt.
☐ Your ability to capitalise on your strengths and to minimise the effect of your weaknesses.

Preparing for an interview in such a way will prove to be time well spent as many franchisors spend a great deal of time during the interview process trying to discover, through the applicant's life experience, whether these attributes are present. The following case study shows how carefully this is undertaken by franchisors:

Les Gray, Chairman, Chemical Express:

We're looking for a certain 'thing' – not a background or education but personal characteristics. I spend time talking to the individual. This will mean three two-hour interviews. The 'thing' we are looking for tends to be drive, energy, commitment, tenacity, but you only discover this if you spend time with them and discover how they have coped in the difficult times as well as the good. You learn about their character and are able to discover if they have the strength of character to build a successful business. A skilful franchisor needs to get under the skin of the individual when choosing.

Interestingly, Mr Gray points to the backgrounds of his five most successful franchisees to illustrate the diversity of career experience and the fact that previous career is not necessarily the most important key to success:

☐ postman;
☐ sales manager;
☐ buyer;
☐ farmer;
☐ shipping agent.

Molly Maid also spends time assessing franchisees. Operations Manager Richard Maidment explains: 'Franchisees are normally selected by interview with the Chief Executive Pam Bader and myself. We have considered the use of aptitude/personality testing but have rejected this approach since there is no ideal profile against which to assess candidates.' A flexible approach to finding franchisees is adopted at Molly Maid because the company has learned that franchisees possess a variety of relevant qualities and characteristics. However, specific personal qualities pinpointed by Molly Maid include 'competence', 'common sense' and 'the right attitude'. Other qualities looked for include:

☐ the ability to relate well to both customers and staff;
☐ full-time commitment;
☐ a sensitive approach to management;
☐ a capacity for hard work and the 'will to succeed'.

The swing to favouring personal attributes is illustrated in the latest NatWest/BFA survey. Personal attributes such as 'self-motivation' are clearly more highly regarded than business experience, with experience in selling and marketing falling by 15 per cent over five years.

A prospective franchisee will need to demonstrate that he has the characteristics that franchisors list highly within the 'attitude' section if he is to succeed in being offered a franchise territory. That 89 per cent list 'self-motivation' as being important might provide a good start in thinking about examples that can demonstrate this characteristic during the interview process.

Experience/Attitude	All franchisors				
	1993 %	1994 %	1995 %	1996 %	1997 %
Experience:					
Selling and marketing	47	32	42	51	32
Other aspects of business	44	27	30	45	31
This industry	20	24	19	28	19
Self-employment	21	17	16	25	4
Don't specify	22	39	41	28	44
Attitude:					
Self-motivated	89	88	98	95	89
Financially aware	85	73	86	84	63
Hard worker	84	84	91	91	71
Hands on/Owner-operator	79	69	77	73	45
Don't specify	1	4	1	4	4
(More than one answer possible)			Source: NatWest/BFA survey		

DEMOGRAPHICS

In the same way that franchisors have changed in order to look for less tangible personal attributes than business experience so too have attitudes to age and gender. In 1993, 49 per cent of franchisors did not have a preference for the age of franchisee. This had risen significantly to 81 per cent by 1997. Likewise, gender specification has also changed with the times. In 1993, 56 per cent didn't specify a preference. This rose to 83 per cent in 1997.

Interestingly, a preference for husband and wife teams has also dropped by 20 per cent. However, franchisors such as Chemical Express do still request that the partner is present during the interview stage, even if they are not to be involved practically in the running of the business. 'We need to see if the applicant has the support of their partner in making the decision. It's not a question of practical support but of moral support,' explains Mr Gray.

Molly Maid reflects the more flexible attitude to the age, gender and background of franchisees: 'There is no typical Molly Maid franchisee. People who run Molly Maid franchises come from all walks of life, ranging from former corporate middle managers to women returning to work. Around two-thirds of Molly Maid franchise owners are women. Some franchisees run their businesses single-handedly while others share the management role with husbands or wives.'

The fact that the majority of Molly Maid franchisees are women suggests that while franchisors are quite flexible about the typical applicant profile, the franchisees are self-selecting and tend to go for industry sectors that have been gender specific.

Comparing the last five years of NatWest/BFA statistics reveals the most significant change to have been that the percentage of franchisors looking for franchisees in the 31–40 age group has dropped by 35 per cent; furthermore, the group that states that it does not specify a desired age range at all has also dropped by 32 per cent. Again, this might well reflect the trend across industry that has recognised that the worst excesses of 'downsizing' in the 1980s, which left many over-fifties unemployed, in reality lost companies invaluable experience which is not easily replaced through the fast-track training of younger members of staff.

Demographics	All franchisors				
	1993 %	1994 %	1995 %	1996 %	1997 %
Age:					
Up to 30	11	9	11	10	5
31–40	42	29	21	18	17
41–50	28	23	19	19	12
Over 50	10	10	16	4	2
Don't specify	49	66	71	75	81
Gender:					
Men	25	20	7	5	10
Women	13	14	2	3	8
Husband and wife teams	30	25	11	11	10
Don't specify	56	67	83	84	84
(More than one answer possible)	Source: NatWest/BFA survey				

Indeed, those that had the skills and know-how to train the next level of employees were often the very people that had been made redundant! It appears then that franchisors are far more flexible than in previous years about age, gender and whether franchisees are husband and wife teams.

FRANCHISEE PROFILES

While franchisors are adapting their criteria in the search for suitable candidates perhaps the biggest clue is to look at the characteristics of franchisees who have successfully completed the application process. Interestingly, the most recent NatWest/BFA survey suggests that while franchisors have changed their selection criteria, franchisee profiles have remained remarkably stable during the last five years. Over half of all franchisees are between 30 and 50 and the vast majority are male, married and have qualifications of some sort or other. Whether this will change over the next five years, only time will tell. However, it is clear that franchisors are now far more willing to look at a range of characteristics and experiences to find the right franchisee.

Successful selection might well depend on the chemistry between an applicant and interviewer. Being aware of what a skilful interviewer is looking for will help create that chemistry and bring out the best in the potential franchisee by being prepared to produce examples that might not be immediately obvious and which could be from other areas of life. Franchisors differ markedly in the success rate of applicants going on to become franchisees. In the case of Molly Maid, 80 per cent of interviewees go on to run franchises. On the other hand, Chemical Express only offers franchises to 30 per cent of those that they interview. Being able to understand what the franchisor is looking for will greatly enhance your chance of being selected and should prepare the ground for developing a good working relationship for the future.

7 | Training Opportunities

People are a business's most valuable asset. Often the only difference between one company and another is the people – their products and services are all but identical. You only have to consider the car hire business to see the truth in that statement. The cars, hire prices, contracts and even their respective advertisements in the Yellow Pages are nearly identical. They all service city centres, airports and main railway stations.

The 'difference' only becomes apparent when someone answers your telephone call:

- [ ] How long do they take?
- [ ] Do they sound pleasant and professional – or hostile and bored?
- [ ] Do they have information at their fingertips – or do they say they will call you back, and then never do;
- [ ] Do they take the time to understand your needs, and propose alternatives if they don't have exactly what you asked for – or do they just try to foist any car onto you?

Try phoning any three car hire firms, hotels or plumbers, or walking into any restaurant, print shop or exhaust-fitting centre. The chances are their 'products' are not what determines whether or not you buy from them. But the people do make the difference.

If a business is only as good as its people, it follows that the people must be good. To be good at anything, you must train, train and then train some more. The often quoted, but nevertheless true statement, attributed to a world number one golfer, 'The more I practise the luckier I get' is a maxim that holds good for business, too.

Big business has long recognised the need for continuous training. In the pharmaceutical industry, for example, a new salesman would spend six months being trained in product knowledge, selling skills and time management, before being unleashed to look after his own territory.

Small businesses, too, have to adopt this zeal for training if they hope to compete, but there is not much evidence that they have. Nearly 40 per cent of all small firms spend one day or less each year being trained. By contrast 88 per cent of large firms spend one day or more on training each year. In fact, big business generally runs more universities than the United States, and has a bigger management education budget than all the business schools combined.

In a franchise you have, to some extent, the best of both worlds. Here you are part of a big organisation, but delivering a local product or service personally.

Many big franchise companies take training so seriously that they too run their own universities. McDonald's has its own university, but it is not only the very biggest franchisors that make such a substantial investment in people, as the following examples illustrate:

> *Big O Tires*, founded in 1962, opened a fully operational training store in Mesa, Arizona in 1993. The facility, now known as the 'Big O University', takes every new franchisee through a five-week intensive programme. Classes start at about 6.30 am daily!
>
> *Subway*, the fast sandwich franchisor, runs the University of Subway at Milford, Connecticut – known in the area as USMC. Their initial programme includes 90 hours of intensive training for new franchisees.

In the European context, using the name 'University' for what is in effect an in-company training facility may sound pretentious. Nevertheless, it sends a clear signal that training people is a prestigious occupation in their company.

When deciding what franchise to take, you need to see what your franchisor has on offer in terms of training. But whatever their strengths or shortcomings in this respect, the final responsibility rests with you. You need to find out what training support the franchisor offers; cajole them to initiate training where they have gaps; and find other ways of training yourself and your team, to make good their shortfalls.

BEFORE TAKING A FRANCHISE

Before taking a franchise it would make sense to find out if 'working for yourself' is likely to suit your skills and temperament. Chapter 5, Evaluating Yourself, gives an insight into how to go about this process.

Next you will need to acquire a broad range of basic business skills. Some of these you may bring with you from previous employment. But if you do not understand cash flow, profit and loss accounts, budgeting, business planning and so forth, it makes good sense to do so before you start in business.

You will also need to know about franchising itself, before you start up. Franchising is not exactly the same as starting your own business. You are, among other things, bound by a contractual relationship with a franchisor, from the outset. This industry knowledge is considered so vital that the International Franchise Association (IFA) runs a 3,500 credit programme (roughly equivalent to a diploma course) leading to the award of Certified Franchise Executive (CFE). The programme covers a broad spectrum of subjects, including franchise law, marketing, finance, employee and franchisee relations, operations and much more.

The British Franchise Association launched a 'Certificate in Franchise Management' in April 1998. The 'BFA Franchise Certificate' demonstrates the need for high standards in many different skills in order to run a franchised business. The certificate is based on the Management Charter Initiative (MCI) standards at NVQ Level 3. The one-year course calls for 4–6 hours of work-based study per week and is designed for groups of participants who undertake the training together, with both open access and in-company courses available. The standard fee is £1,600 per candidate. BFA members already committed to the pilot programme include Greenalls, Select, Cash Generator, Interlink Express, Oscar Pet Foods and Blazes Fireplaces.

Participants take an introductory module plus 5 core modules, each one divided into two phases – a 5-week training phase and a 5-week assessment phase. Training is undertaken through open learning material accompanied by a one-day workshop for each of the modules. Included with the course material is an innovatory set of NVQ competency activities. By completing the activities, candidates will produce evidence of their competence, to the relevant NVQ standards:

Module subjects include:

- [ ] understanding the ethical, legal and marketing aspects of the industry;
- [ ] establishing the franchisor-franchisee relationship;
- [ ] personal effectiveness;
- [ ] interpersonal skills;
- [ ] coaching and counselling skills;
- [ ] time and stress management;
- [ ] team building;
- [ ] motivating;
- [ ] handling conflict;
- [ ] appraising and rewarding teams;
- [ ] financial and business planning;
- [ ] costing and budgeting;
- [ ] profit, loss and balance sheets;
- [ ] developing a business plan;
- [ ] managing operations;
- [ ] identifying problems;
- [ ] legislation in the workplace;
- [ ] developing the business;
- [ ] selling and marketing;
- [ ] customer service;
- [ ] personnel planning and recruitment.

Two qualifications are available on successful completion of the programme: an NVQ Level 3 in Management; and a Certificate in Franchise Management from Nottingham Business School. Holders of the certificate will be eligible to progress to the first stage of the MBA degree.

AFTER TAKING A FRANCHISE

Once you have decided on your franchise it will quickly become apparent which are the most important areas in which to become proficient (or even more so, if you already have some relevant skills).

Selling ability is more or less mandatory for every type of franchise. While you may not be the 'sales type', your 'selling' skills can nevertheless be sharpened by training. By identifying the elements of a successful sale, finding out what the customer wants, matching your product/service to their needs, overcoming objections, gaining agreement and finally closing the sale you can see in which areas training could help you to do better. Even good salespeople are often deficient in listening skills!

One owner-manager, when reviewing the skills he absolutely required of his salespeople, decided self-reliance and a sense of personal responsibility were mandatory. Product knowledge and selling skills he could add later by training – but the other attributes were either there or, in his opinion, could not be added later. Marketing, advertising, sales promotion, budgeting, forecasting, business tax and analysing business data are all other areas in which any self-employed person needs a high level of proficiency.

THE TEAM

Working for yourself does not mean you have to work alone. If you are successful – and in some cases even from the very outset – you will have others working for you. Indeed, until you have built up a team your venture will be fragile, risky and perhaps not that profitable.

As one successful entrepreneur said: 'The key to success is to make other people happy to make you rich.' The table below, culled from the DTI statistics for the UK, makes the point eloquently.

Number of employees in firm	Turnover per employee (£000s)
The boss only	28
1–9	86
10–99	156
100–499	367
500+	209

Turnover growth

It is also interesting to note that these 'efficiencies' tail off sharply once a business has more than 500 employees.

However, that is all some way off for most start-ups. The important task at the outset is to bring in the appropriate people – which means you, the boss, may need to sharpen up your recruitment and selection skills. Then your new employees will need to be quickly and efficiently induced into the way things are done in your business. They will certainly need training in product knowledge, and perhaps in other skill areas, too. You will then need to be able to motivate, communicate, manage, reward, appraise, control – and perhaps even discipline or fire staff. Each of these is a possible subject for training.

TRAINING METHODS

Training is not only delivered in classrooms. Subway's initial training programme, for example, includes about 55 hours of classroom instruction and 35 hours of in-store work. The types of training you can consider are grouped under the following three headings.

On-the-job

This is the name given to most types of training that happen in the workplace. You may have seen those irritating notices in your building society's window, for example, saying 'Closed until 9.30am for staff training.' What one hopes is happening during these sessions is that junior staff are being given instructions and advice by more experienced staff in how to become better at their jobs. Coaching is a less obstructive form of on-the-job training. Here a boss watches an employee at work, then takes a few minutes out to show them how they could have done the job better. Then they watch again, and keep offering advice and training until the task is performed to a satisfactory standard. But to be effective, coaching has to be done well. Otherwise it ends up being seen as criticism, or worse still, nagging.

So if you are going to get the best out of coaching you need to be trained yourself. The advantage of on-the-job training is that it is relevant, immediate and consumes few resources.

Off-the-job

This is the general name given to courses of instruction held in colleges, by training companies or by the franchisors' instructors. Off-the-job training has the advantages of being sure of the students' full attention (or at least has that opportunity) and of using professional instructors.

But taking people off work can be expensive and disruptive. A variant that tries to get around this problem is to bring the instructor to your premises. But with only 2 or 3 people to train this could prove expensive. One way around this is to club together with other local employers with similar training needs, and use your premises for the training. Communication and telephone skills are pretty universal requirements, and could respond well to this treatment.

Next-to-the-job

These are training methods that can be done without leaving your work premises (or can be done in private time), but cannot be done while working. These include: Distance Learning Programmes, books, videos and computer-based training programmes using CD ROMS and the Internet.

American franchisor Management Recruiters International (MRI) has introduced video-conferencing into its training. MRI's business depends on getting the right candidate to an interview with the right company, a process that required a lot of flying around the country. Each year it put 90,000 people onto aeroplanes to be interviewed – until it began to use video-conferencing. Now MRI uses video-conferencing to deliver training. MRI University, its training function, delivered 8,632,000 student hours in its first 14 months of operation.

INFORMATION TECHNOLOGY AND THE INTERNET

One area where few people are sufficiently knowledgeable is IT. Even the most experienced of us needs constant training to keep up to date with this rapidly changing field.

For franchisor and franchisee alike, IT is changing the way business is done. Examples of things that can be done using the Internet have been identified by Simon Collin:

☐ carrying out research before you launch a new marketing campaign;
☐ checking patents, demographics or statistics on a new sales area;
☐ researching new manufacturers and distributors;
☐ creating a new way of marketing your products to a niche group of users;
☐ keeping in touch with your customers and employees;
☐ keeping in touch with the office when you travel;
☐ cutting long-distance phone bills.

Source: *Doing Business on the Internet*, Kogan Page Ltd

Further reasons for undertaking training in this area are as follows:

Effective research

The information superhighway provides the opportunity to thoroughly research your market in a number of ways. Using search engines you can browse company Web sites, look at various news services and newspapers and join user groups and newsgroups to get feedback on ideas or products. Furthermore, through the Internet you can subscribe to mailing lists to reach customers, and keep them up to date by e-mail.

Using e-mail

Using e-mail you can, as suggested above, access the thousands of mailing lists available on the Internet. Furthermore, if your work involves travelling, e-mail is an invaluable tool for keeping in touch with the office. Automated responses to sales enquiries, telephoning, video-conferencing, distributing documents to salesforces and keeping in touch with customers are all uses of e-mail that have been adopted by business.

Enhancing market strategy

Using the Internet to market a product or service has also become popular with business, and creating your own Web site is an effective way to meet new customers. Secure ways of paying over the Internet have now been developed and have created the opportunity to trade electronically.

Here are some examples of how leading American franchisors are using IT to give their business, and that of their franchisees, a competitive edge.

Sylvan Learning Systems has been providing children and adults with supplemental education and computer-based training since 1979. Recently, it started to produce training videos for its franchisees, but a year later it saw that satellite programmes would be more cost effective. Franchisees pay $25 a month for six hours of weekly programmes that include lectures and seminars from industry experts.

Padgett Business Services does accounting for small businesses, and provides timely financial information. Changes in tax laws and so on have to be communicated to franchisees quickly. Once information was printed and went out by post, fax or on diskette. Now it goes out on the company's Web site. Franchisees download the very latest information – daily if need be. Padgett's support team answers franchisees' queries via modem direct from their Web site.

A Shade Better has introduced a point-of-sale till system that not only does end of day tallies, but provides sophisticated and timely marketing data. It tracks customer spending patterns, monitors trends in product sales, line by line, monitors margins and keeps track of inventory levels. It saves franchisees' time and helps them make better business decisions.

It is possible that franchisors will have in-house training on a regular basis to keep you up to date with Information Technology. Most will have adopted modern ways of communicating within their systems and will inevitably pass these on as an integral part of the franchise package. However, should you be expected to possess this knowledge independently there are many short training courses available about the Internet.

The Information Society Initiative is a partnership between government and business to help small and medium-sized companies try out technologies such as the Internet, e-mail and video-conferencing. Each centre offers services tailored to local needs, with the emphasis in every case on applications that can be put into immediate and effective use. To find out where your nearest centre is contact the ISI Business Info Line (tel: 0345 152000).

Using IT effectively requires you and your staff to have a good grounding in what is available and what it can do for your business. It is a rich and fertile area for training.

THE TRAINING PLAN

Nothing worthwhile in business should be undertaken without a plan, and training is no exception. The training plan needs to be built around the business objectives. So two questions need to be answered before training begins:

☐ What is our business and what makes us stand out from the crowd – and what will make us stay ahead?

☐ What skills, knowledge and abilities are needed now and in the future, to ensure we can continue to meet and exceed the needs of our customers and stay ahead?

From that analysis the training plan should cover the following points:

☐ Who is to be trained?

☐ In which subjects will they be trained?

☐ What changes in performance will be delivered by undergoing that training?

☐ How much is it worth to get people to the new skill/knowledge level?

☐ How will we monitor training effectiveness, ie are we getting what we paid for?

☐ Who are the best people to deliver training?

☐ What is the most appropriate training medium?

☐ When should that training start and finish?

That most training is perceived by the recipients as 'boring, irrelevant, a total waste of time, but at least a change from work', is because much of the training is undertaken on a whim. An interesting leaflet, newspaper article or book prompts a particular line of thought – and the first affordable course that covers that area is bought.

Even if your franchisor is providing 'free' training, you should have your own training plan. Bad or just plain irrelevant training is time-wasting, demotivating and counter-productive. You may consider, as part of your plan, introducing National Vocational Qualifications (NVQs). These are designed to be rigorous, but practical and relevant to the organisation's need. The attraction of an NVQ is that, as with any other examining body, there is an absolute standard of performance against which to measure an employee's achievement, set by an independent, authoritative and respected body.

HELP AND ADVICE

Business Links are a one-stop contact point for small businesses, providing signposting to all aspects of help and advice. Each Business Link is aware of the training programmes and providers in its area.

The Institute of Directors, local Chambers of Commerce and the Industrial Society are all organisations involved in running their own programmes. Many of these are targeted at the self-employed and those working in small businesses.

The BBC book, *The Complete Small Business Guide*, lists the colleges and universities that provide courses for those in small businesses, and gives a brief description of the types of training programmes on offer.

Once your franchise is established, you will need to give thought to its expansion. You may want to add similar franchises to your network. For example, many Body Shop franchisees own several shops. But you could consider expanding in quite different directions. The Cranfield School of Management's Business Growth Programme is intended to help successful business proprietors explore ways of making their business even more prosperous.

Part Three:

Setting Up

8 The Franchise Contract

The obligations of the franchisee and the franchisor, all the rules and limitations governing the way the business is conducted, as well as the conditions under which it may be terminated by either party, are incorporated in the franchise agreement. It goes almost without saying, therefore, that every line of this document ought to be scrutinised very carefully before the franchisee commits himself to its contents by signing it. Indeed, it is essential that he should go through it with a solicitor, having first made a note of any points which he wishes to query, either because he does not understand them or because he disagrees with the conditions they impose.

The general advice of those experienced in franchise matters is to beware of the franchisor who is prepared to haggle to any substantial extent over the terms of the contract. If a clause was not reasonable in the first instance, why was it there at all, having regard to the fact that trust between franchisor and franchisee is essential if the deal is to work? If that trust does not exist, the possibility is that there may be future differences over meanings of the fine print. Once the agreement is signed it becomes much more difficult to argue over what has been contracted. Thus the general recommendation is that, unless there is a broad measure of agreement over terms, and their meaning is clear and acceptable to both parties, it is better not to go ahead at all.

All contracts, naturally, differ somewhat between companies and the type of franchise involved, but they also have quite a number of features in common. In fact a franchise sometimes involves signing two agreements: a purchase agreement and the franchise agreement itself.

THE PURCHASE AGREEMENT

This is a fairly short document which simply states that, subject to the franchisor finding a suitable site, the franchisee will enter into the contract set out in the franchise agreement – provided, of course, that the prospective franchisee has read and approved that document within a reasonable time. Given that condition, a sum is paid to the franchisor's solicitors as part of the initial fee. This gives the franchisor the go-ahead with his search for a suitable site, which includes not only investigating its commercial viability but also finding out whether consents and planning permission would be available for its intended use. If no suitable site is found in a given time, the deposit is returned to the prospective franchisee; but if he rejects the site or changes his mind in the interim, then the deposit is forfeited.

THE FRANCHISE AGREEMENT

This is a much longer document. Not necessarily in this order, it covers:

1. The nature and name of the activity being franchised.
2. The franchise territory.
3. The term of the franchise.
4. The franchise fee and royalty.
5. What the franchisor agrees to do.
6. What the franchisee undertakes to do.
7. The conditions under which the franchisee may sell or assign the business.
8. The conditions under which the franchisee may terminate the franchise and what his obligations are in that case.
9. The terms and obligations of the franchisor in similar circumstances.

The nature and name of the activity being franchised

This is simply a standard set of clauses which describes the franchise and warrants that the franchisor has a right to it and its associated trade marks, methods, receipts, specifications and whatever else is involved. The franchisee should, of course, be aware that the franchisor cannot guarantee protection from competition by similar products that are not franchised or which are part of some other franchise.

The franchise territory

The franchise will normally be a protected or privileged right to operate in a certain territory, best shown on an actual map or defined by the use of postal codes. The problem is that this is hard to enforce fully because there is virtually nothing that can be done to prevent a franchisee from a neighbouring territory trading in yours, even though he may not be allowed a physical presence there. The questions to ask, therefore, are:

1. How close is the nearest outlet of the same franchise and how many such franchises are located in that general area?
2. If a franchise is being offered in an adjacent territory, will you be given first refusal?
3. Can the territory be reduced by the franchisor, and if so under what conditions?
4. Who has chosen the territory? If the franchisor has made the choice, on what basis was it made? Has there, for instance, been an independent market survey and has it vindicated the franchisor's claims for the territory's viability?

The term of the franchise

This is the duration over which the franchise runs. The franchisee should have an option to renew the franchise at the end of this period for a similar length of time, though he may be asked to give warning of his intent to do so before then. About one in five franchisors ask for a renewal fee at the end of the contract period, though the terms of the extension of the franchise should be similar to those under which the franchise is operating at present or, at any rate, no less favourable than those under which new franchises are being offered. Other points are:

1. The franchise usually runs for at least five years although the average is seven. But the critical point to watch is that it lasts long enough for you to get the start-up costs back. Remember that you may be involved in considerable investment in equipment as well as the franchisor's initial fee.
2. Complications can arise over leased premises. Does the lease run for the same length of time as the franchise? If you have a ten-year lease and a seven-year franchise, what restrictions are being placed on you from trading at the same premises in another capacity?
3. If the premises are part of the franchise deal, you should check whether you have any obligations to make repairs at the end of the term. The costs involved could be considerable.

The franchise fee and royalty

The clauses under this heading set out when the initial payment is due and how much it will be. Equally important, it establishes the royalties due to the franchisor – the percentage, how it is calculated, how often it is paid, whether advertising is treated separately, and what proofs the franchisor requires that the amount remitted to him is correct. There are obviously many things to watch out for here and the advice of an accountant and a solicitor might well be opportune.

1. A low royalty rate is not necessarily a favourable sign, particularly when it is combined with a high start-up fee. It could mean that back-up and services from the franchisor will not be adequate. It could even mean that he is interested in nothing much more than taking your start-up fee and running with it!
2. Since the royalty is usually based on sales turnover rather than profits, the franchisor may press to increase volume at

the cost of profitability. The two are by no means necessarily the same.

3. Ideally there should be a royalty rate reducing as volume grows. It is also a good thing if the start-up fee is payable in two instalments – eg part on signature of the contract, the rest when you commence business.

4. A low royalty rate may also be balanced by the franchisor putting an excessive mark-up on goods and services which the franchisee is obliged to buy. It is important to find out whether such 'hidden extras' operate.

5. The conditions of the franchise may allow you to sell other goods and services – for instance, you may have a deep freeze from which you can supply non-franchised food and drink. In that case you should establish whether royalties are due on all takings or only on those relating to the franchise.

6. It is also important to ensure that where royalties are paid on sales, these are net of VAT.

7. Where relevant, the agreement must state whether royalties are paid on amounts invoiced, or only on those actually paid for.

8. When the franchisor generally undertakes to devote a proportion of the fees to advertising, the question arises, what proportion? And is it devoted to promoting the franchise as a whole, or your particular one? Or a mixture of both, and if so, in what proportion? When a separate percentage is charged for advertising, you will also need to be reassured on these points.

9. If interest is due on late payments, is the rate reasonable?

10. If a minimum monthly payment is laid down, is it a fair figure?

What the franchisor agrees to do

The question of advertising may well be covered under this heading, but it is plainly an important issue since, to a large extent, the 'established name', which is an essential part of the business format, is promoted in this way. Other aspects that should be included under this section of the agreement are:

1. Training. What is offered? Who pays for it? How long does it go on for? If training is a prerequisite for the franchisee and/or his staff, who pays for it and what happens if either of them fails? If staff need to be trained, the same question has to be asked.
2. Site selection and layout. Is assistance provided? If so, at what additional cost?
3. Specifications for premises and equipment. The franchisor will probably lay down certain quality controls in providing this service as well as demanding uniformity with other franchises in the group.
4. The provision of promotional and other advertising material. The question that arises here as well as in 3. is the extent to which this is useful in your particular franchise, assuming it has to be paid for. One of the main points of friction between franchisor and franchisee is when the latter is committed to acquiring point of sale material or bits of 'styling' or equipment which he may not feel he needs or does not like.
5. The operating manual. As stated earlier, it is important that this document should be intelligible.
6. Where the franchisor supplies goods and/or services to the franchisee, these should be fairly priced. It is equally important that, should there be any delays and hold-ups in supply, the franchisee should be free to purchase elsewhere.
7. Normally the franchisor should provide assistance during the opening period and also pledge himself to provide back-up, support and help, as and when it is needed over a wide range of matters – trouble with the product or its preparation, staff training, book-keeping, negotiations with local authorities etc.

Undertakings

Essentially the franchisee undertakes to observe the franchisor's conditions and requirements, so the question to consider is whether these are fair and reasonable.

1. They may include a clause prohibiting the franchisee from trading in anybody else's products or getting supplies from

other sources. What happens if there are unreasonable delays?

2. If selling prices are set by the franchisor, do they provide an adequate margin and are they competitive with similar goods and services obtainable in the area?

3. Are the obligations placed on the franchisee as regards standards of equipment, age and condition of vehicles, decor, and participation in national or regional sales promotion or training exercises fair, or do they constitute a hidden cost?

4. Are the operating procedures contained in the manual simple to follow and practical or are they complex and burdensome?

5. Are there any unreasonable conditions which would prevent you carrying on some other trade for any period of time should you wish to discontinue the franchise at the end of the term, or indeed before then?

6. Are there any unreasonable conditions which would prevent you from getting the best price for the franchise should you want to sell it?

Selling or assigning the business

The extent to which you are free to sell or assign the business at its market value (preferably assessed independently) is a measure of the freedom or control you have over it. If you cannot sell except to the franchisor, or unreasonable obstacles are placed in the way of your disposing of it to a third party, its value will be greatly diminished and in extreme circumstances the effort you have put into building up the business might be negated completely.

Most franchise agreements will lay down, first, that you will give the franchisor first refusal in the event of your wishing to sell or assign the franchise; second, that any third party you want to sell to has to be approved by the franchisor. It is natural that he should want to impose that condition, since he would want to be sure that the new franchisee is acceptable to him and that he is a fit person, financially and in every other respect, to run the operation.

Problems would occur, however, if the franchisor were to demand an excessive start-up or transfer fee from the new franchisee or high royalties. At best, it would reduce the amount he would pay you for the franchise. At worst, an unscrupulous franchisor could effectively block any disposal, except on his terms. It is important that the question of transfer is covered in a way acceptable to you, even if at the moment it is far from your intention to dispose of the franchise. Sadly, the question of death or disability cannot be ignored altogether.

Termination by the franchisee

There is no sense in holding someone to a franchise against his will, but the agreement should specify that the franchisee can terminate it before the set date. Apart from such considerations as illness, it could be that the business fails to make a sufficient income for its owner or simply that he does not like that kind of work.

Often a minimum period of time is laid down before the agreement can be terminated before the due date from causes within the control of the franchisee and he may also have to give notice of intent in writing in such cases. The starting-up fee will, of course, be forfeited but the point to watch is that there are no other financial penalties; for instance, an obligation to compensate the franchisor for loss of income should it prove impossible to find another buyer for the business.

Another potential problem is stock in trade and equipment. If you cannot sell them on the open market upon termination, will the franchisor buy back from you and, if so, on what terms?

Termination by the franchisor

The obvious reasons for the franchisor to terminate an agreement before its end would be if the franchisee failed to comply with its conditions, which makes it doubly important that you, as franchisee, should read this document carefully and satisfy yourself that you understand it and are able to comply with it. However, specific circumstances for termination should be set out in the agreement – beware of any that conceal them in the fine print. There should also be a period of grace in which you are given the chance to put right any faults the franchisor has pointed out to you.

He may, however, spell out circumstances which he regards as so serious a breach of the agreement as to justify termination without notice: consistent failure to report sales if the franchise royalty is based on percentage (as it usually is); failure to stay open for business over a prolonged period; trading in goods which are not part of the franchise without the franchisor's permission; acts which are prejudicial to the good name of the franchisor – all these are examples of what might reasonably be called material breaches of contract.

Conditions which you should question, however, and which have been known to appear in agreements, are:

1. A requirement, as a condition of the agreement, to purchase minimum quantities of goods or services from the franchisor or some source nominated by him.
2. A stipulation that certain sales quotas are reached (unless you are absolutely certain that these are feasible).
3. An open-ended obligation to commit yourself to expenditure on goods or services or equipment, ie one that is not related to a realistic level of profitability.
4. Anything described as a 'material' breach of the agreement which in your opinion or that of your advisers is in fact a trivial one.
5. Any clause which places a penalty on you other than the franchisor's legal costs in the case of a dispute and the loss of the franchise itself should a premature termination be enforced. In other words, anything you have paid for should remain your property and you should be free to dispose of it at whatever price you can get for it, unless the franchisor agrees to buy it back at market rates.
6. Any restrictive covenants which may try to stop you from setting up a competing business should you eventually decide to strike out on your own. Such covenants are hard to enforce in the courts, but they can involve you in delays and legal costs.

While no reputable franchisor is out to gain an unfair advantage over you in the agreement, it is vital to bear in mind that since he and his advisers have drawn it up, it will tend to favour him rather than you as the franchisee. Do not assume, therefore, that the benefit of the doubt will be on your side, and sign nothing (not even a contract with a 'cooling off period') until you have thoroughly understood it, had any provisions that are not clear explained by *your* advisers, and thought about the implications of every clause in it.

The franchise contract

Checklist:

☐ Are *all* commitments revealed in the earlier questions contained in the contract, ie royalties, fees, franchisor support etc?
☐ How long is the franchise agreement for?
☐ What happens at the end of the contract period?
☐ Do your leases and financing arrangements cover an appropriate time period, bearing in mind the length of the franchise agreement?
☐ What are the conditions for renewing the contract?
☐ Under what conditions, if any, can you assign the franchise?
☐ How can you terminate the contract before the expiry date, for example, if you just don't like the business?
☐ How can the franchisor terminate the contract before the expiry date?
☐ How long do you have to correct any defaults?
☐ Is there an arbitration process?
☐ When terminating the contract for whatever reason, how will you be compensated for any 'goodwill' generated over the life of the contract?
☐ What happens in the event of your illness or death?
☐ Are there any restrictions on what other business activities you can involve yourself in (both during the franchise and after termination)?
☐ How does the franchisor propose to maintain his good reputation and hence yours?
☐ Have you any rights to the franchisor's innovations?
☐ What is your position if the franchisor fails or is put into liquidation?
☐ What happens to stock etc if the agreement is terminated?

9 Financing a Franchise

HOW MUCH WILL YOU NEED?

Starting any business involves financial risks. One serious cause of new business failure is underestimating exactly how much money is needed to get the business going.

This is not surprising when you consider that, for most people, starting up is a once in a lifetime event. Even for the few with experience, their subsequent ventures are rarely both in the same business field and on the same scale as their first. It is all too easy to miscalculate how much premises will cost to convert for your purposes, or exactly how much output you will get from a piece of second-hand machinery.

A further serious cause of financial failure is being too optimistic about your market. This in turn can lead to expecting too much cash in too soon and so underestimating how much working capital you will need to finance stocks, debtors and other overheads. Even when business picks up, young enterprises are often undercapitalised and so unable to fund the growth in sales. In bankers' language they are over trading.

The main financial advantage that a franchisor can provide for a franchisee is an accurate prediction of both fixed and working capital requirements. After all, the franchisors have launched tens and often hundreds of 'new' businesses. Their expertise in the field of 'launch' experience in a particular business area should be second to none.

It is perhaps worth mentioning at this stage one dichotomy

presented by the franchisors' experience at launching outlets (or the lack of it). The well-established and often large franchise organisations use their very success as an argument for franchisees to 'buy-in'. However, the entrepreneurial instinct of the potential franchisee will lead him to look for market gaps, innovations, new ideas and potential winners. This will encourage him to look at franchisors who may not have the base of experience needed to make good predictions about franchisees' capital needs.

Case study

One new fast food franchise that opened in Paris will serve as a warning. The franchisor's experience was based on a relatively new building which had many of the facilities required for a food operation already installed. It was also in a thriving Paris area with a good mix of residential and office property nearby. The franchisor sold his first franchise package after only a few months' operation in this pilot unit. His franchisee's premises, though filling all the basic requirements, were an old and ill-equipped building in an exclusively commercial area. Immediately it became apparent that the estimates for alterations and kitchen equipment were hopelessly wrong, and within a few weeks it was clear that his working capital projections were equally over-optimistic. This meant that instead of £30,000 start-up capital, the first franchisee found he needed £60,000. The franchisor was unable to help but fortunately the franchisee managed to raise it by the skin of his teeth, and so survived. But he certainly didn't become rich, except perhaps in experience.

This all makes it extremely important to know as much as possible about the financial structure of the franchisor. We have tried to give you some clues both in Chapter 4 and in the information provided on each franchisor in Chapter 14.

Buying a franchise can cost as much as £300,000. A Holiday Inn franchise would be more again. Even within the same organisation, costs of outlets can vary considerably depending on size and location. Some offer different types of franchise within the same business, also with considerable differences in cost.

Start-up costs

The cost of operating a franchise involves, first, a series of initial costs and, second, various ongoing charges related to the operation of the concern. An initial measure of the importance of the various charges is the extent of their incidence, as reported by franchisors. The average initial outlay for a franchise is £42,800. A typical property-based franchisee will need to invest £53,400, while a home or mobile business will need £34,100. Recurring costs averaging 10 per cent of turnover will also have to be paid.

Recurring franchise costs (1998)		
	Incidence %	Proportion of sales %
Management services fee	72	5.6
Contribution to advertising	57	4.2
Mark-up on supplies	40	10.5
Other charges	37	4.7

These overall average figures mask some quite large variations between franchise systems, many of which can be attributed to the different structures of the franchises concerned.

HOW CAN YOU FINANCE A FRANCHISE?

Financing a new franchise, while no easier than finding funds for any new venture, is at last attracting some heavyweight contenders. About 80 per cent of franchisees borrow to set up, borrowing an average of £29,250 each. Around 84 per cent raised the funds from a bank, while 15 per cent either took out a mortgage or sold a house.* The balance used a wide mixture of funds, including all those listed in this chapter.

Before considering possible sources of finance, we must first look at what we want to do with the money. By that we don't mean refurbishing property or buying a vehicle or getting in

---

* NatWest/BFA survey.

start-up stock. Financial institutions tend to look at money as being either fixed or working capital. *Fixed capital* is money tied up in things the business intends to keep over longer periods of time, such as property, equipment, vehicles etc. *Working capital* is the money used to finance the day-to-day operations. The stock, for example, and any money required to finance your customers until they pay up, are elements of working capital, as are all other running costs and overheads.

Type of capital	Business needs	Financing method
Fixed capital	Acquiring or altering a property; buying equipment, such as cookers, ovens, photocopiers or vehicles; the franchise fee and other 'start-up' package costs such as training.	Your own capital Term loans Hire purchase Leasing Sale and leaseback Venture capital Government loan guarantee scheme Mortgage loan
Working capital	Raw materials or finished goods; money to finance debtors; dealing with seasonal peaks and troughs, expansion or unexpected short-term problems; paying royalties.	Your own capital Bank overdrafts Factoring Trade credit Government loan guarantee scheme

Your own capital

Obviously the first place to start is to find out exactly how much you have to invest in the franchise. You may not have much in ready cash, but you may have valuable assets that can be converted into cash, or other borrowing. The difference between your assets and liabilities is your 'net worth'. This is the maximum security that you can offer for any money borrowed, and it is hoped that the calculations below will yield a pleasant surprise.

YOUR NET WORTH			
Assets		**Liabilities**	
Cash in hand and in bank,		Overdraft	£
building society, National		Mortgage	£
Savings or other deposits	£	Other loans	£
Stocks and shares	£	Hire purchase	£
Current redemption value	£	Tax due, including	
of insurance policies	£	capital gains	£
Value of home	£	Credit cards due	£
Any other property	£	Garage, local shop	
Motor car(s) etc	£	accounts due	£
Jewellery, paintings and		Any other financial	
other marketable valuables	£	obligations	£
Any money due to you	£		
Value of your existing business	£		
Total assets	£	Total liabilities	£

Net worth = Total assets – Total liabilities.

External funds

To most of us borrowing money is synonymous with a visit to our local bank manager. Though not the only sources of finance the banks are a good starting point.

There are over a dozen clearing banks, as the High Street bankers are usually called, and they are in serious competition with each other for new business. It is as well to remember that a bank manager is judged on the quantity and quality of his lending and not on the deposits he takes. If he cannot 'successfully' lend, he can't make a profit himself.

For most satisfactory new business propositions the clearing bankers would normally be happy to match £1 for £1 the money put up by the 'owner', ie 1:1 gearing. Perhaps as an indication of how favourably the banks view ethical business format franchising, they will extend this ratio to two-thirds bank funding to one-third owner's cash, for approved franchise proposals.

They will also recommend a 'package' of funds – part term

loan, part overdraft and perhaps part government loan guarantee – that best suits the type of franchise you are interested in (details of these types of financing are given below). For example, if the franchise you are considering is a service, requiring few physical assets, serving cash customers and expecting to break even in the first year, you may be advised to take a small term loan and a larger overdraft facility. This will most closely match the funds to your needs, minimising interest charges without upsetting the long-term security of the business.

The converse relationship between loan capital and overdraft may be prudent if you are considering a 'capital intensive' franchise, such as a major fast food outlet.

One last point on the clearing banks. Normally your financial relationship with your bank is your business. If North American trends in franchise funding are anything to go by, this may be a thing of the past. There, and in some cases here, banks ask franchisees to sign a release when they advance a funding package. This allows the bank to tell the franchisor if you are exceeding your financial limits.

At least five major banks and several other financial institutions have identified franchising as an important market for them to be in. As well as lending over £150 million to franchisees, they have appointed managers and special departments responsible for looking after the franchise area. These suppliers of finance for franchising are listed in Chapter 15.

These banks can offer both general and specific advice to assist potential franchisees in evaluating a franchise from their considerable database of market and financial information on franchise organisations. For the established franchisee, the banks can provide financial packages tailored to individual needs.

The banks offer a wide range of services in their own right. Through wholly or partially owned subsidiaries, they cover virtually every aspect of the financial market. For franchisees their services include overdrafts, term loans, factoring, leasing and the government loan guarantee scheme. As well as providing funds, the clearing banks have considerable expertise in the areas of tax, insurance and financial advice generally.

Overdrafts

Bank overdrafts are the most common type of short-term finance. They are simple to arrange; you just talk to your local bank manager. They are flexible, with no minimum level. Sums of money can be drawn or repaid within the total amount agreed. They are relatively cheap, with interest paid only on the outstanding daily balance. Of course, interest rates can fluctuate, so what seemed a small sum of money one year can prove crippling if interest rates jump suddenly. Normally you do not repay the 'capital': you simply renew or alter the overdraft facility from time to time. However, overdrafts are theoretically repayable on demand, so you should not use short-term overdraft money to finance long-term needs, such as buying a lease, or some plant and equipment.

Term loans

These are rather more formal than a simple overdraft and cover periods of up to three, three to ten and ten to twenty years respectively. They are usually secured against an existing fixed asset or one to be acquired, or are guaranteed personally by the directors (proprietors). This may involve you in some costs for legal fees and arrangement or consultants' fees, so it may be a little more expensive than an overdraft, but unless you default on the interest charges you can be reasonably confident of having the use of the money throughout the whole term of the borrowing. The interest rates on the loan can either be fixed for the term or variable with the prevailing interest rate. A fixed rate is to some extent a gamble, which may work in your favour, depending on how interest rates move over the term of the loan. So, if general interest rates rise you win, and if they fall you lose. A variable rate means that you do not take that risk. There is another benefit to a fixed rate of interest. It should make planning ahead a little easier with a fixed financial commitment, unlike a variable overdraft rate, where a sudden rise can have disastrous consequences.

The banks are becoming quite venturesome in their competition for new and small business accounts. One major clearer has a scheme which offers free banking to new businesses for one year – even if they are overdrawn – provided the limit has been agreed.

The key innovation is that the loan will be subordinated to other creditors, with the bank repaid before the shareholders but after all the other creditors if the company failed. In return for this risk they are likely to want an option on up to 25 per cent of the company's capital.

We strongly recommend you take professional advice before entering into any financial commitments.

Public sector

The government encourages the financing of new and small firms in a number of ways. One source of funding is the **Small Firms Loan Guarantee Scheme**:

☐ The scheme guarantees loans from banks and other financial institutions for small businesses with viable business proposals which have tried and failed to obtain a conventional loan because of a lack of security.

Loans are available for periods of between 2 and 10 years on sums from £5,000 to £100,000 (£250,000 in the case of businesses which have been trading for more than 2 years). The DTI guarantees 70 per cent of the loan (85 per cent in the case of businesses trading for more than 2 years). In return for the guarantee the borrower pays the DTI a premium of 1.5 per cent per year on the outstanding amount of the loan. The premium is reduced to 0.5 per cent if the loan is taken at a fixed rate of interest. A recent addition to this scheme aims to help stimulate venture capital for businesses with growth potential. The Enterprise Fund will inject at least £20 million over the next three years.

The commercial aspects of the loan are matters between the borrower and the lender.

☐ *Eligibility criteria*
New and existing UK companies with an annual turnover no greater than £1.5 million (£3 million in the case of manufacturers). Many business activities are eligible but there are a number of exclusions. Loans are available for most business purposes although there are a number of restrictions.

☐ *How to apply*

All applications are made direct to one of the scheme's lenders. There are currently 19 lenders:

3I Group plc	Midland Bank
Bank of Ireland	National Westminster Bank
Bank of Scotland	Northern Bank
Barclays Bank	Northern Investors Loan
Clydesdale Bank	Finance Ltd
Co-operative Bank	Royal Bank of Scotland
Doncaster Business Advice Centre	TSB Group
First Trust (Allied Irish)	Ulster Bank
Lloyds Bank	Yorkshire Bank
London Enterprise Agency (Lenta)	Yorkshire Enterprise Ltd

Further information is available from any of the scheme's lenders or from:

Small Firms Loan Guarantee Section
SME Policy Directorate
Department of Trade and Industry
Level 2
St Mary's House
c/o Moorfoot
Sheffield S1 4PQ
Tel: (0114) 259 7308/9
Fax: (0114) 259 7316
e-mail: David.Moore@SFSH-Sheffield.dti.gov.uk

Sources of loan finance – a summary

Three-fifths of franchisors assist their franchisees in raising their initial investment. Of those that do, over 90 per cent help arrange the start-up finance, usually via a bank. Nearly 10 per cent actually supply the finance themselves. Turning to the franchisees, 52 per cent borrowed money to set up.

The average amount borrowed in 1997 was £29,000. There were sectoral differences in borrowing requirements. Ninety-four per cent of franchisees in the quick-printing, copying and graphic design sectors had to borrow money because of the high capital costs of equipment. Retail franchisees are most likely to borrow

Source of loan (more than one source possible)	All borrowing franchisees 1997 %
Bank	76
Building society	8
Friends/relatives	9
Finance house	1
Franchisor	3
Other	3
Value of loan	
Up to £10,000	28
£10,001–£50,000	58
£50,001 plus	14

money (63 per cent), and borrowed the largest amounts (£42,500). The table above summarises loan amounts and sources.*

Factoring

This is only available to a franchise that invoices other business customers for its services. ServiceMaster, for example, who clean carpets and upholstery, have both domestic and commercial clients. So it may be possible to factor the commercial invoices.

Factoring is an arrangement which allows you to receive up to 80 per cent of the cash due from your customers more quickly than they would normally pay. The factoring company buys your trade debts and provides a debtor accounting and administration service. In other words, it takes over the day-to-day work of invoicing and sending out reminders and statements. This can be a particularly helpful service to a small expanding business. It allows the management to concentrate on expanding the business, with the factoring company providing expert guidance on credit control, 100 per cent protection against bad debts, and improved cash flow.

You will, of course, have to pay for factoring services. Having the cash before your customers pay will cost you a little more

---

* NatWest/BFA survey.

than normal overdraft rates. The factoring service will cost between 0.5 and 3.5 per cent of the turnover, depending on volume of work, the number of debtors, average invoice amount and other related factors. You can get up to 80 per cent of the value of your invoice in advance, with the remainder paid when your customer settles up, less the various charges just mentioned.

If you sell direct to the public, if you sell complex and expensive capital equipment or expect progress payments on a long-term project, factoring is not for you. If you are expanding more rapidly than other sources of finance will allow, this may be a useful service. All other things being equal, it should be possible to find a factor if your turnover exceeds £25,000 per annum, though the larger firm will look for around £100,000 as the economic cut-off point.

The Factors and Discounters Association is at the Administration Office, 2nd Floor Boston House, The Little Green, Richmond, Surrey TW9 1QE (tel: 0181 332 9955). FDA members charge between 0.75 and 2.5 per cent of gross turnover for the sales ledger package, and around bank overdraft rate for finance charges. They will advance about 80 per cent of the invoice price almost immediately the invoice is raised. They generally only consider customers with £100,000 per annum turnover, but may consider good cases from £50,000.

Leasing

This is a way of getting the use of vehicles, plant and equipment without paying the full cost at once. Operating leases are taken out where you will use the equipment for less than its full economic life – for example, a car, photocopier, vending machine or kitchen equipment. The lessor takes the risk of the equipment becoming obsolete, and assumes responsibility for repairs, maintenance and insurance. As you, the lessee, are paying for this service, it is more expensive than a finance lease, where you lease the equipment for most of its economic life and maintain and insure it yourself. Leases can normally be extended, often for fairly nominal sums, in the latter years.

The obvious attraction of leasing is that no deposit is needed, leaving your working capital for more profitable use elsewhere.

Also, the cost is known from the start, making forward planning more simple. There may even be some tax advantages over other forms of finance. However, there are some possible pitfalls, which only a close examination of the small print will reveal. So do take professional advice before taking out a lease.

Information is obtainable from: The Finance and Leasing Association, Imperial House, 15–19 Kingsway, Holborn, London WC2B 6UM (tel: 0171 836 6511).

Hire purchase

This differs from leasing in that you have the option at the start to become the owner of the equipment after a series of payments has been made. The interest is usually fixed and often more expensive than a bank loan. However, manufacturers (notably car makers) often subsidise this interest, so it pays to shop around both for sources of hire purchase finance and manufacturers of equipment.

The Finance Houses Association, address and telephone number as for the Finance and Leasing Association, can provide you with a short list of companies to approach.

Mortgage loan

This operates in the same way as an ordinary mortgage. The money borrowed is used to buy the freehold on the business premises. That then acts as the main security for the loan with regular repayments made up of interest charges and principal, paid to the lender.

The main suppliers are the insurance companies and pension funds, who generally prefer to deal in sums above £50,000. Some of the smaller companies will lend as little as £5000, particularly if the borrower is a policy-holder. As well as the regular payments, a charge of about 2 per cent will be made to cover the survey, valuation and legal work in drawing up agreements.

Sale and leaseback

This involves selling the freehold of a property owned by a business to a financial institution, which agrees to grant you a lease on the premises.

The lender will want to be sure that you can afford the lease, so a profit track record will probably be needed, and all expenses involved in the negotiations are met by the borrower. The borrower then has the use of the value of the asset in immediate cash to plough into the business.

The tax aspects of sale and leaseback are complex and work more in the favour of some types of business than others, so professional advice is essential before entering into any arrangement.

As with other forms of finance, it is a competitive market and it is worth getting a few 'quotes'.

Trade credit

Once you have established creditworthiness, it may be possible to take advantage of trade credit extended by suppliers. This usually takes the form of allowing you anything from seven days to three months from receiving the goods, before you have to pay for them. However, if your franchisor is your main source of supply, you may have very little flexibility in this area.

Even if you have a choice, you will have to weigh carefully the benefit of taking this credit against the cost of losing any cash discounts offered. For example, if you are offered a 2.5 per cent discount for cash settlement, this is a saving of £25 for every £1000 of purchase. If the alternative is to take six weeks' credit, the saving is the cost of borrowing that sum from, say, your bank on overdraft. So if your bank interest rate is 16 per cent per annum, that is equivalent to 0.31 per cent per week. Six weeks would save you 1.85 per cent. On £1000 of purchase you would save only £18.50 of bank interest. This means that the cash discount is more attractive. However, you may not have the cash or overdraft facility, so your choice is restricted.

Venture capital

This is the start-up capital usually associated with businesses involved in technological and technical innovation. The sums involved are usually up to £100,000 over periods of five years or more. 3i (Investors in Industry), the major providers of venture capital in the UK, has £3.5 million invested in individual franchises. With this capital usually comes management expertise, often in the form of a board member from the financial institution. So you would have to be able to work with him, and probably give a personal guarantee for the sums involved.

IMPROVING YOUR CHANCE OF GETTING EXTERNAL FINANCE

Not having enough ready cash to finance buying a franchise will force you to look to one or more of these external sources of finance for the balance of your funds. At first glance this may appear to be a disadvantage. Nothing could be further from the truth. A hard critical look at your business proposal by an outsider is exactly what you need. To have a serious chance of raising money you will have to marshal all the facts about the franchise proposal yourself, and understand them well enough to communicate clearly to a third party. Simply having a good 'net worth' is unlikely to be sufficient in itself to secure a loan. This examination by an outside professional will certainly prompt you to ask your prospective franchisor some searching questions.

The National Westminster Bank has produced a useful checklist to help you get your loan proposal together. Not every heading is appropriate to a franchise proposal but the great majority are. Working your way through this checklist will certainly improve your knowledge and understanding of the franchise proposal itself; and it will improve your chances of reaching a satisfactory outcome to your search for funds.

If you are looking for a substantial injection of external funds, you will need to prepare a business plan. Kogan Page's *The Business Plan Workbook* by Colin Barrow, Paul Barrow and Robert Brown, third edition revised 1998, is a comprehensive guide to researching and writing your own business plan.

Checklist:

About you

- [ ] Brief synopsis for your own banker, detailed for approach to others: age, education, experience.
- [ ] Personal means, eg property, liabilities, guarantees. Other business connections.
- [ ] For a type of business new to you, or start-up situation, outline experience, ability and factors leading up to your decision.

Your business

- [ ] Brief details of when established, purpose then and now, how the business has evolved, main factors contributing to progress.
- [ ] Reputation, current structure and organisation. Internal accounting system.
- [ ] Past three years' audited accounts if available, and latest position.
- [ ] Up-to-date profit and loss figures, including details of withdrawals.
- [ ] Up-to-date liquid figures, ie debtors, creditors, stock, bank balance etc.
- [ ] Borrowing history and existing commitments, eg HP, leasing loans. Bankers.
- [ ] Description of major assets, and any changes.

Your key personnel

- [ ] Age, qualifications, experience, competence, of directorate/senior management. Directors' bankers.
- [ ] Emergency situation, someone to run the business in your absence.
- [ ] List of principal shareholders/relationships.

Your purpose

- [ ] Explain fully your business plan, the use to which the money will be put, eg expansion, diversification, start-up.
- [ ] Describe the practical aspects involved and the how and when of implementation.
- [ ] Diagrams, sketches, photographs etc are usually helpful, eg property purchase and conversion to your use.
- [ ] Consider: planning permission, legal restrictions, government policy.
- [ ] Contingency plans for set-backs: reliability of supplies/raw

materials/alternative sources, other factors outside your control, eg weather.
- ☐ Relevance to existing operations, opportunity for shared overheads, disruption of current business.
- ☐ Personnel: are more staff required, availability of specialist skills/training? Management ability for expanded/different operation?

Your market
- ☐ Estimated demand, short- and long-term. External verification of market forecasts, eg from trade associations, market research publications.
- ☐ Competition, who from, likely developments.
- ☐ Describe your competitive advantages, eg quality, uniqueness, pricing (justify), location – local/national.
- ☐ Marketing included in costings?
- ☐ If new, or technology based, or highly specialised business – detail and perspective necessary.
  NB A banker does not need to know how it works (though he may be interested), just that it does, is reliable, and has good sales prospects.

Your profit
- ☐ Demonstrate how profits will be made, include detailed breakdown of costings, timing, projected sales, orders already held.
- ☐ Profit projections should attempt to cover the period of a loan, however sketchy.
- ☐ For capital investment – profit appraisal. Capital allowances, eg new small workshop scheme.
- ☐ Everything included in costings, eg tax, stamp duty, legal fees, bank interest?

The amount
- ☐ State precisely the amounts and type of finance required and when it will be needed. Is type of finance correct, eg overdraft to finance working capital, term loan for capital expenditure?
- ☐ Is the amount requested sufficient, eg increased working capital requirements/margin for unforeseen circumstances?
- ☐ Detail the amount and form of your contribution to the total cost.

☐ Justify all figures – cash flow forecast for next 12 months: show maximum range. All outgoings considered, eg net VAT, holiday pay, bank interest and repayments, personal drawings.

Repayment
☐ Relate projected profitability and cash flow to expected repayments. Justify fully the term requested: is it long enough?
☐ How quickly will the business generate cash? Is a repayment 'holiday' necessary and what turnover needs to be achieved to break even?
☐ Consider the worst situation, feasibility of contingency plans, irretrievable losses.
☐ Interest rate – effect of variation in base rate.

Security
☐ What assets are/will be available as security?
☐ Are any assets already used for security elsewhere?
☐ Independent/realistic valuation of assets offered. Leasehold considerations, any unusual features/saleability. Support for guarantees.
☐ Agreement of other interested parties/realistic awareness of loss of asset.
☐ Insurance: life, property, business.

© National Westminster Bank plc

Even if the first financial institution you approach turns you down, don't despair. Ask why and profit by their explanation. Sometimes would-be borrowers have had different answers from different branches of the same bank.

FRANCHISOR HELP IN RAISING MONEY

A few years ago you could have expected your franchisor to do little to help you raise finance.

The past few years have seen a dramatic reversal. Indeed, it is probably true to say that if a franchisor cannot put his potential franchisees in contact with a financial institution for at least some of the money needed, there is something very suspicious about the franchise proposition.

For the lender of money, the business format franchise provides almost unparalleled security.

Any request for funds poses two problems for the lender. Is there a market for the product or service the business is going to offer? Is the person thinking of setting up the business suitable and appropriately skilled for the job? Normally the lender has to use his own unaided judgement to answer these questions, but with a franchise the position is much clearer. In most cases there are enough Body Shop or Dyno-Rod outlets to establish the market viability of the product or service and the franchisors themselves will both vet and train the franchisee. These factors can alter the balance of risk in the lender's favour.

Many franchisors have now established close relationships with financial institutions, and can provide a comprehensive financial package for potential franchisees.

THE CONSUMER CREDIT ACT

When this Act came into force in May 1985 banks were forced to review their policy on lending to lower priced franchises. The effect has been to cause several of the banks to raise their minimum lending figure to £15,001 because of a technical legal liability to the lender on loans under £15,000 to sole traders and partnerships.

ENTERPRISE INVESTMENT SCHEME

The **Enterprise Investment Scheme (EIS)** is intended to make it attractive for private individuals and pools of funds to invest equity capital in small firms.

The EIS replaced the Business Expansion Scheme on 1 January 1994. The EIS is available for new equity investment in qualifying UK unquoted trading companies, whether or not they are incorporated and resident here and to investors liable to UK income tax, whether or not they are resident here.

Its main features are:

- [ ] Income tax relief at 20 per cent on investments up to £150,000 per annum.
- [ ] Capital gains tax exemption on disposal of shares.
- [ ] Relief for a loss on disposal either against income or capital gains tax.
- [ ] Investor(s) can be paid directors and still qualify if not connected with the company or its trade before eligible shares were issued.
- [ ] No investment limit per company per annum.
- [ ] Minimum holding period of five years.
- [ ] Investment must be in an unquoted trading company carrying on a qualifying activity for a minimum of three years.
- [ ] Companies invested in must have no more than £10 million maximum assets value before investment and £11 million after.
- [ ] Unlimited deferral relief where chargeable gains are invested in eligible shares.
- [ ] Up to £25,000 of investment made by an individual can be carried back to the previous year, if made in the first half of the tax year.

The scheme does not extend to investment in property development, farming, market gardening, forestry, hotels, guest houses and residential homes.

These notes are a guide to the scheme as it presently operates. The government makes changes to the scheme fairly frequently, so to see if your company could be eligible as an EIS investment vehicle you would need to speak to your accountant and to the Inland Revenue.

10 Legal, Tax and Employment Considerations

THE LEGAL FORM OF THE BUSINESS

Well before you start trading you will need to consider in what legal form you wish to run your business. For a potential franchisee there are only three likely possibilities, as certain structures such as workers' co-operatives are unlikely to be appropriate. These three possibilities, together with the percentage of franchisees adopting that form, are:*

Franchisee business status					
	All franchisees			1997 turnover	
	1996	1997	Up to £49K	£50–199K	£200K plus
	%	%	%	%	%
Sole trader	55	53	89	57	39
Partnership	22	19	7	26	15
Limited company	23	28	4	16	46

Each of these forms has certain advantages and some drawbacks which should be considered before you make a decision.

---

* NatWest/BFA survey

Sole trader

The sole trader is the original form of entrepreneur. You put in your own money as the risk capital, you take all business decisions, and you take all the profits. The drawback to this independence is that you also have to suffer any losses in their entirety.

If you are a sole trader there is no legal distinction between you and your business – your business is merely one of your assets, just as your house or car is. It follows from this that if your business should fail the creditors have a right, not only to the assets of the business, but also to your personal assets, subject only to the provisions of the Bankruptcy Acts which allow you to keep only a few absolutely basic essentials for yourself and your family. In other words, if the business goes down, everything you own – house, car, jewellery, furniture, savings – can be seized and sold to pay off the creditors.

To a certain extent it is possible to avoid these consequences by ensuring that your private assets are the legal property of your wife or husband rather than yourself. The creditors have a claim only against your assets, not against your spouse's. Before you decide that this is the answer to any possible problems you should consider the following:

1. You cannot pass over the property when you realise you are running into trouble. The transfer must be made at least two years before, and while you are still solvent (ie able to meet your debts as they fall due). As most business failures occur in the early years this probably means making the transfer before you take out the franchise.

2. In order to be effective, the transfer must be absolute – you cannot retain an interest in or control those assets. Therefore you have no power to dictate what your spouse does with them, and must consider carefully the degree of trust you place in your husband or wife and the stability of your marital relationship. You may have to decide whether you have more faith in your spouse or your own business acumen!

In return for the drawbacks, you have the pleasure of being entirely your own boss, subject only to your agreement with your franchisor, and you have very few legal formalities with which to comply, compared with a limited company. In fact, apart from regulations particular to your business (eg fire and health regulations for a fast food franchise), you may only encounter problems in keeping the records required for the Customs and Excise and for your accountant to negotiate your liability to tax with the Inland Revenue.

Partnerships

Partnerships are effectively collections of sole traders and as such share the legal problems attached to personal liability. Two points in particular merit attention:

Disadvantages

1. Your partner may make a business mistake, perhaps by signing a disastrous contract, without your knowledge or consent. If this happens, the business as a whole can still fail, and your personal assets be taken to pay the creditors even though the failure was no fault of yours.
2. If your partner goes bankrupt in his personal capacity – for example, in his private life he may have a tendency to fast women and slow horses – his share of the partnership is one of his assets, and his creditors will want to realise the cash from this. Obviously, you as a private individual are not liable for his private debts, but the requirement to buy him out of the partnership or to find someone to buy his share could prove fatal to the business.

Advantages

1. By pooling resources you will have more capital.
2. You have someone with whom to discuss problems and strategies.
3. Your home life may be easier as there will not be the same pressure on you to be there all the time – you can split responsibilities.
4. You can contribute different personalities, experience and talents.

5.   It will be less of a disaster if you are ill.

Most of these advantages do not have the same force if your prospective partner is your spouse. When considering whether to take in your spouse as a partner, or merely have him or her help-ing (paid or otherwise), you should consider these points:

☐   While you are starting up it may help your peace of mind to know that you have a spouse in steady employment outside the business, so you are assured of at least a basic income.

☐   If your spouse is a partner in the business you cannot protect your assets by transferring them into his or her name.

☐   You should keep firmly in mind that one in three marriages now ends in divorce. Although statistics are not available, it is probable that the proportion is even higher among owners of newly started businesses because of the additional strains. If your spouse is a partner, you cannot get rid of him or her eas-ily, and few people would relish the thought of having to run a business in partnership with someone they were in the process of divorcing! In most cases it is better to have your spouse as an employee. (See also the comments on taxation on pages 112–17.)

Assuming that you have decided that a partnership is right for you, the legal requirements are dealt with in the Partnership Act 1890. In contrast to modern protective legislation, this Act, framed in the spirit of Victorian self-help, assumes that competent busi-nessmen should know what they are doing, and merely provides a framework of an agreement which applies *in the absence of agree-ment to the contrary*. Any of the arrangements can be varied according to the wishes of the partners. The main provisions are:

☐   All partners contribute capital equally.
☐   All partners share profits and losses equally.
☐   No partner shall have interest paid on his capital.
☐   No partner shall be paid a salary.
☐   All partners have an equal say in the management of the business.

These provisions may suit you perfectly well, but it is likely that you will want to vary some of them. In any case you would be well advised to get a *partnership agreement* drawn up in writing by a solicitor, because even though you can have a perfectly legal agreement established verbally or just based on how you have been conducting the business, there is always the problem of evidence in the event of an argument.

A possibility to guard against is *accidentally* finding yourself in partnership with someone. Because there is no necessity for a partnership agreement to be in writing, or for any legal formalities, you may find yourself in a situation where you are held to be in partnership even though that was not the original intention. For example, if an employee (your spouse, perhaps) commonly negotiated with full authority, signed cheques, and was paid according to the level of profits he might well be held to be in partnership, particularly if his name appeared on the firm's stationery. None of these things would be decisive in itself, but in combination they might lead any person dealing with the business reasonably to suppose himself to be dealing with a partner.

Limited liability companies

As the name suggests, in this form of business your liability is limited to the amount you contribute by way of share capital. The essential point to realise is that the company is a separate legal entity – it has a legal personality which is quite distinct from that of the shareholders. It follows from this that if the business should fail, the creditors can only have a right to the assets of the business; they cannot demand any more from the shareholders than the amount of share capital they have contracted to take up – if they have already paid that in full there is no further recourse.

BASIC TAX ISSUES

Important as the question of the legal form of the business may be, many of the questions of liability arise only in the case of business failure. Taking a more optimistic viewpoint, tax considerations are more important when the business is making a profit.

It must be emphasised that taxation is an extremely complicated area, and one that changes very rapidly, so this section can give only a very broad outline of the main considerations.

The basis of taxation

Business profits (whether sole traders/partnerships or limited companies) are taxed according to the rules of Schedule D Case I or II. (I relates to profits from a trade, II to income from a profession or vocation – there are no important differences.) Your taxable profit is computed by taking your profit according to the accounts and adjusting it. The adjustment is necessary because the normal rules for preparing a set of accounts are not the same as those in tax law, which means that your *accounting* profit will often bear very little relation to your *taxable* profit. An accountant's help is vital here if you do not wish to pay more tax than you legally must.

You are allowed to set an expense against your income if it is:

1. Incurred *wholly and exclusively* for the purposes of trade.
2. Properly charged against income (not, for example, purchase of a property lease, which is capital).
3. Not specifically disallowed by statute (for example, you cannot set entertainment of customers against your tax, although it is a perfectly legitimate accounting expense).

It is beyond the scope of this book to detail all the expenses which are and are not allowable; good, clear summaries can be found in the books mentioned in Chapter 15, page 232. The following points should, however, be noted carefully:

1. If you do some of your work at home you can normally set a proportion of your rent, rates, light, heat and telephone bills etc against your business income.
2. If your wife cannot work outside the home (perhaps because there are young children) she can be an employee and be paid up to £4,195 a year (1998/99) which will be deducted from your profits but will not be taxable on her. It is necessary to convince the Inspector of Taxes that she does actually do work for the business to this value, and that it is paid to her.
3. If you are a sole trader or partnership your tax is assessed

effectively a year in arrears, except in the first two or three years, when the profits earned in the first year or 18 months determine the liability. For this reason it is vital that your taxable profits in this first period should be as low as legally possible (a loss is preferable) as this will affect your tax payable for three years.

Note: this does *not* apply to limited companies.

4. Choose your *accounting date* carefully. Deciding when your business started trading is rarely a clear-cut decision. Often business expenses were incurred months and even years before the first cash came in. Left to their own devices, most people prepare their first accounts for a 12-month period, based either on the calendar or tax year. They mistakenly think that administrative tidiness or convenience are the only factors to consider. That is not so. There is an opportunity to influence the timing of cash flow in the business's favour. This sort of advantage can often mean the difference between success and failure in the first year. Look at the two cases below:

> Business A decides on 31 March 1991 as the end of its first financial year. Half of the tax on the profits is due on 1 January 1992 and the balance on 1 July 1992, so tax is paid an average of 12 months after the profits have been made. (31 March 1991 to 1 January 1992 = 9 months; 31 March 1991 to 1 July 1992 = 15 months; (9 + 15) ÷ 2 = 12 months.)
>
> Business B, however, decides to have 30 April 1991 as the end of its first financial year, as this is after the end of the Inland Revenue's tax year, which ended on 5 April 1991, so tax is not due until 1993. Half is paid on 1 January 1993 and the balance on 1 July 1993. This means an average of 23 months elapses before tax is paid, giving an extra 11 months' interest-free credit.

This cash flow benefit is created by the simple expedient of choosing the best first year end for a particular business.

This example is something of an over-simplification and other factors will come into play. It will not, for example, apply to new limited companies which all have to pay tax a flat nine months after their year end, whatever that date is, but it does serve to illustrate the potential benefits to be gained by using professional advice.

5. Any further difference in treatment between sole traders and limited companies as far as tax is concerned relates to the treatment of *losses*. If you are a sole trader (or partnership) your income from the business is just one of your sources of income, and is added to any other income you and your wife may have. Similarly, as it is your aggregate income which is important, any business losses can be set against your other income. So if your wife earns £8000 a year as a teacher and has had PAYE deducted of (say) £1800, and your business makes a loss of £4000, then assuming you have no other income, the two will be netted off and you will have a joint income of only £4000 against which you will set the married man's allowance and the wife's earned income relief so you will be able to reclaim most of the PAYE. The relief in the opening years is even more generous – if you make a tax loss in any of the first four years of the business you may reclaim some or all of the tax you or your spouse has paid in the preceding three years. Neither of these loss reliefs applies to limited companies; a limited company is a separate legal person, so the profits belong to the company, the company has its own tax liability, and, most important, the losses are 'locked into' the company; you cannot set company losses against your own other income. This is the other side of the coin of limited liability – if you wish to take advantage of the protection provided for your personal assets by operating the business through a separate legal entity, you cannot also treat that entity's losses as your own and benefit from them.

6. If you are a limited company you will take remuneration as director's remuneration. As you are technically an employee of your company, tax should be paid under PAYE, and also National Insurance Class I contributions are due – both employer's (the company) and employee's (yourself). This can prove very much more expensive than the Classes 2 and 4 paid by a sole trader.

7. Unless you take out the entire profits as director's remuneration, the balance will be taxed at *corporation tax* rate of 21 per cent on profits up to £300,000 rising to 33 per cent on profits

over £1.5 million. The rate of corporation tax is fixed annually by Parliament in the Finance Act for the preceding financial year.

8. Expenditure on plant and machinery qualifies for writing down allowances on a 25 per cent reducing balance basis. It may therefore make more sense in some circumstances to lease than to buy outright (the cost of leasing can be set against tax).

9. Do not let the tax tail wag the commercial dog! In other words, you are in business primarily to make profits, not to avoid paying tax. Your primary concern should be with the business; do not make decisions purely to save tax.

Purely from a tax point of view, most businesses are better off starting as sole traders or partnerships for the cash flow reasons mentioned earlier. It is also much simpler to start off as a sole trader or partnership and to incorporate when necessary than to try to do the procedure in reverse.

Despite the tax advantages to being a sole trader, particularly at low levels of profit, you may feel that the protection of your private assets by operating as a limited company is well worth the tax disadvantages – much depends on your personal circumstances and your attitude to taking risks.

Finally, it should be realised that in revenue law the onus of disclosure and proof is on the *taxpayer*. In criminal law you are innocent until proved guilty, but for tax purposes you are liable until you prove otherwise. Moreover, it is your responsibility to notify the Inland Revenue of taxable income, not for the Inspector to ask (though he eventually will). Remember, *ignorance of the law is no excuse*.

10. The position on *leased assets* is somewhat different. You do not own the asset, the lessor does. He, therefore, is entitled to claim the writing down allowances and this benefit to him is reflected in the lower rental figure that he can then charge. Whether outright purchase or leasing is beneficial will depend on the individual business and the anticipated profits. If finance is not available, however, there may be no choice but to lease. One point to note is that if there is an option to purchase the asset after a certain period, the Inland

Revenue may not regard the transaction as a genuine leasing arrangement, but as a form of credit sale. Again, this is not necessarily a disadvantage; it all depends on the pattern of profits and professional advice should be sought.

Value added tax

VAT is complicated tax. Essentially, you must register if your taxable turnover, ie sales (*not* profit), exceeds £49,000 in any 12-month period. The general rule is that all supplies of goods and services are taxable at the standard rate (17.5 per cent) unless they are specifically stated by the law to be zero-rated or exempt. In deciding whether your turnover exceeds the limit you have to include the zero-rated sales (things like most foods, books and children's clothing) as they are technically taxable; it's just that the rate of tax is 0 per cent. You leave out exempt items. There are three free booklets issued by the Customs and Excise: a simple introductory booklet called 'Should you be registered for VAT?' and two more detailed booklets called 'General Guide' and 'Scope and Coverage'. If in doubt (and the language is not easy to understand) ask your accountant or the local branch of the Customs and Excise; after all, they would rather help you to get it right in the first place than have to sort it out later when you have made a mess of it.

Each quarter, you will have to complete a return which shows your purchases and the VAT you paid on them, and your sales and the VAT you collected on them. The VAT paid and collected are offset against each other and the balance sent to the Customs and Excise. If you have paid more VAT in any quarter than you have collected you will get a refund. For this reason it sometimes pays to register even if you don't have to – if you are selling mostly zero-rated items for example; also, being registered for VAT may make your business look more workmanlike and less amateurish to your potential customers.

PROFESSIONAL ADVICE

You will need the services of an accountant or lawyer, preferably someone you have chosen yourself because otherwise you can never be quite sure that his advice will be impartial. For a small business such as franchising, it is better to go to the more modest High Street type of professional who knows local circumstances and by-laws (as well as possibly having some inside information on people you will be dealing with), rather than to a big, centrally located firm.

You will also need to make sure that *insurance* is fully taken care of. Normally, the franchisor will see to it that this is done, but since the business is effectively yours, the responsibility for it rests on you. The main kinds of cover you will need are:

1. Insurance of your premises.
2. Insurance of the contents of your premises.
3. Insurance of your stock.
4. Employer's liability if you employ staff on the premises, even on a part-time basis.
5. Public liability in case you cause injury to a member of the public or his premises in the course of business. You will also need third-party public liability if you employ staff or work with partners.
6. Legal insurance policies to cover you against prosecution under Acts of Parliament which relate to your business (eg those covering unfair dismissal and fair trading).
7. Insurance against losing your driving licence, important if your business depends on your being able to drive.

The National Federation of Self-Employed and Small Businesses now includes automatic legal insurance in its membership subscription. This covers professional and legal fees of up to £50,000 for appeals to VAT tribunals, defence of Health and Safety at Work prosecutions, 90 per cent of the cost of an Industrial Tribunal Award and defence of private and business motoring prosecutions. The NFSE also runs a voluntary top-up scheme to supplement this basic legal cover.

EMPLOYING PEOPLE

Franchising has the feature, somewhat unusual in business start-up situations, that in many cases – certainly where retailing and fast food are concerned – it is necessary to begin looking for staff at a fairly early stage. This will bring the owners into sharp contact with a number of problem areas with which they may previously have been mercifully unfamiliar. Apart from the difficulty of finding Mr or Ms Right – a task which even experienced personnel people admit in their more candid moments is something of a lottery – a mass of legislation has been enacted in recent years which, it is thought by some, has favoured the rights of employees at the expense of employers. The aim of this legislation has been mainly to protect the workforces of larger companies from arbitrary hiring and firing, as well as to take account of the special problems of racial minorities at work and the changes in public opinion about women's rights. However, it also touches even the smallest employer in almost equal measure to large ones and it covers most part-time as well as full-time employees.

Franchisees are likely to be particularly affected, not only because they often employ workers who fall into all these categories, but because the rules of the franchise may impose conditions which have a great deal of bearing on the employer–employee relationship, and which are actually laid down by the franchisor: for instance, the way employees who come into contact with the public are expected to dress. Even though such rules may have been imposed by the franchisor, when it comes to a dispute involving unfair dismissal, the franchisee cannot hide behind the terms of the franchise. Unfair dismissal, though, is only one of several issues involved. Whole books could be and have been written about the legal technicalities, but all we can do here is draw the reader's attention to the fact that there are major pitfalls to avoid when employing people.

Issues involved in employing people:

☐ unfair dismissal;
☐ redundancy;
☐ health and safety;
☐ equal opportunities;
☐ disability discrimination.

The contract of employment

The contract of employment statement which has to be issued in writing to every employee who is going to work for you for 16 hours or more per week within 8 weeks of joining is in fact not a pitfall, but a rather sensible document which clarifies right from the outset what the terms of employment are. From the employer's point of view, the necessity of drafting a contract of employment statement should concentrate the mind wonderfully on issues about which it is all too easy to be sloppy at the expense of subsequent aggravation, such as hours of work, holidays and, above all, exactly what it is the employee is supposed to be doing. The following points have to be covered in the contract, and you must say if you have not covered one or other of them:

☐ The rate of pay and how it is calculated.
☐ Whether it is paid weekly or monthly.
☐ The normal hours of work and the terms and conditions relating to them.
☐ Holidays and holiday pay entitlement.
☐ Provision for sick pay.
☐ Pensions and pension schemes.
☐ Notice required by both parties.
☐ The job title.
☐ Any disciplinary rules relating to the job.
☐ Grievance procedures.

If there is any change in any of these terms, the employee has to be notified of this fact in writing, within a month of the change having taken place.

Recruitment

The cost of discharging staff, whether because of redundancy or dismissal, makes it imperative that you should make the right decisions in picking people to work for you in the first place. Personnel selection can be described as a gamble but there are ways in which you can cut down on the odds against you.

The most obvious question to ask yourself is whether you really do need to take someone on permanently at all. The principle that is often put forward for the purchase of equipment – never buy anything outright unless you are sure you have a continuing use for it and that it will pay for itself over a reasonable interval of time – also applies to personnel. The legal constraints that cover part-time or full-time employees do not extend to personnel from agencies or outside work done on contract, and this could well be the best way of tackling a particular problem, such as an upward bump in demand, until you are sure that it is going to last. It is worth remembering, too, that when you take on staff you take on a good many payroll and administrative overheads in addition to their salary. These can add quite significantly to your costs.

Sooner or later, though, if you want your business to grow (and growth of some kind seems to be an inevitable concomitant of success) you are going to need people. But even then you should ask yourself what exactly you need them for and how much you can afford to pay. Clarifying these two issues is not only important in itself, but it will also give you the basis of a job description which you can use in your press advertising or approach to a recruitment agency, at the interview and, finally, in the contract of employment. Around it you should also build a series of questions to ask the interviewee that should give you some indication of his competence to do the job. Such questions should call for a detailed response rather than a 'yes' or 'no' type of answer. For example, if you are interviewing a waitress, asking her whether she has worked in that capacity before will tell you something, but not nearly as much as asking where she has worked and for how long she was employed in each earlier job.

Asking job applicants to fill in a simple application form, stating age, qualifications, experience, the names of referees, and any other questions you would like answered (and can legitimately ask) is a good employment practice. It will give you some idea whether the person concerned can deal with simple paperwork; furthermore, people seem to be more truthful in writing than in a face-to-face interview.

Competence is part of the story. Equally important is the interviewee's track record: how many previous employers he has had and whether his progress has been up, down or steady. Too many job changes at frequent intervals can be a bad sign and it is fair to ask searching questions about this if it is part of the employment pattern. It is also wise to be cautious about people who are willing to take a large drop in salary. Even in these days when good jobs are less easy to come by (at least in some parts of the country) you ought tactfully to find out what the reason is.

Health is another important point to check on because dismissing people on medical grounds is very difficult, though there is no obligation to take them on in the first instance. For this reason some employers ask all job candidates to fill in an application form on which, among other questions, that of health is raised. Clearly if the applicant had misled you on the state of his health, that would materially weaken his case at a tribunal. What can be done to establish whether he has any commitments in the way of public or trade union duties which might affect his ability to work the hours required is a much more difficult issue. Putting anything to him in writing would, no doubt, produce an outcry, so perhaps such questions should only be raised verbally, if at all.

Possibly the references will give you a clue and you should always ask for and check references. They are not always reliable – most employers are reasonable people and they will not speak ill of an ex-employee if they can help it (though they should be aware that it is illegal to misrepresent the abilities or overstate the capability of an employee or ex-employee to another employer) – but they will generally alert you to real disaster areas. Telephone reference checks are widely reckoned to be more reliable than written ones because referees are nearly always more forthcoming in conversation than in a letter, since the law of libel and industrial relations law looms large in any written deposition.

Part Four:

Current Opportunities

11 Current Franchises – a Guide

Finding out about the franchise opportunities on offer is a costly and time-consuming business. Any attempt to provide a complete guide to current franchise opportunities in the UK, or perhaps anywhere, would be difficult. The present state of the UK franchise market, with new franchisors being 'born' every few months, makes such a guide a daunting task.

This guide has been compiled from responses to our postal survey. Almost every current business category of franchise is included. Whether you are looking for a particular market, size of franchise organisation, cost of entry, product or service, industrial or consumer market based franchise, you will find it here. The guide provides a useful framework within which you can evaluate new franchisors as they bring business concepts to the market place.

WHY LOOK AT FRANCHISOR COMPANIES ANYWAY?

Much of the detail of the guide looks at the franchisor's organisation rather than simply at the franchise opportunity on offer. We think that in evaluating a business proposal both the proposer and the proposal are equally important subjects for analysis. Indeed, unless you know something of the former, it is very difficult to estimate the substance and credibility of the latter.

Your view of the merits of any advice would be influenced by the qualifications and experience of the adviser. A twice bank-rupted and down-at-heel stranger would not command quite the same respect for his business proposal as, for example, a million-aire industrialist.

What has to be remembered is that successful 'business format' franchising requires much more than just a good, or even a unique, idea or product. What a franchisee is buying is the fran-chisor's capability of 'reproducing' success with a good (or unique) product or service. So prospective franchisees need to be able to see something of the substance (or otherwise) of the fran-chisor's company because it is that organisation that holds the key to whether or not the franchise chain can be securely devel-oped for mutual profit.

WHAT SHOULD YOU LOOK AT?

Most of the content of this book is intended to give you a clearer under-standing of franchising and the specific questions to ask a franchisor.

In the opportunities guide we have tried to summarise the key information that you need to help you make decisions, not deci-sions about whether or not to invest in a particular franchise, but decisions on which ones to pursue further. It is extremely impor-tant to take appropriate professional advice before committing yourself and your funds to any franchise agreement.

The information in this guide is given in sections.

Company and business profile of each franchise

A summary sheet is given for each franchisor setting out facts in the following way:

The name of the franchise organisation is given first, together with a description of its business, whether or not it is a BFA mem-ber, number of franchise outlets, year started, capital required and management fee for start up.

We have told you whether or not the franchisor is a *member of the British Franchise Association* whose members are listed on pages

205–17. The BFA is the UK's self-regulating body for business format franchising. It has rules for membership which in themselves tell you something about the franchisor. However, it must be pointed out that many very reputable companies are not members of the BFA, just as the same is true, for example, of the Confederation of British Industries.

For obvious reasons the costs associated with each franchise can only be an approximate figure. Within each franchise there can be several different types or size of franchise on offer, and the costs are subject to alteration over time. Certainly the relationship of the initial fees to royalties is an important consideration. You should be suspicious of anyone offering a very 'front loaded' contract; that is, asking for a very high fee and a very low or non-existent royalty. There may be a sound reason. For example, the franchisor may supply the 'goods' and take a margin on these. Although a possible source of irritation later on, the royalty fees are one sure way of maintaining the franchisor's commitment to developing the business, and providing good advice and support in the future.

COMPANY AND BUSINESS PROFILE OF EACH FRANCHISE

Some major franchisors are not listed in this directory because they did not respond to our survey. Responses have been published in good faith. However, any listing here is not an endorsement by us or the *Daily Telegraph*.

AAC Auto-Air Conditioning
Unit 53, Commerce Court
Cutler Heights Lane
Bradford
BD4 8NW
Tel: 01274 669966
Fax: 01274 668000
e-mail: n/a
Web site: n/a
Contact: D Langley

Business description: Auto air conditioning
BFA membership: No
No. of franchise outlets: 6
Year business started: 1995 (started franchise 1998)

Start-up capital (minimum): £13,500
Initial fee: £8,000
Management fee: 12.5%
Proportion of start-up capital that can be arranged: 80%

Additional information: Repair and service of auto air conditioning units. Installation of Sp. 11- A/C units to shops, offices, commercial business. Service repair and maintenance.

Action Bikes plc
3–5 St John's Road
Isleworth
Middlesex
TW7 6NA
Tel: 0181 560 9494
Fax: 0181 758 9368
e-mail: n/a
Web site: n/a
Contact: Ian Johnstone

Business description: Franchise cycle shops
BFA membership: No
No. of franchise outlets: 50
Year business started: 1991 from a core family business established in the 1930s

Start-up capital (minimum): £59,300
Initial fee: £9,500
Management fee: 6% plus 1.5% advertising/marketing
Proportion of start-up capital that can be arranged: 70%

AIMS Partnership plc
3 Park Road
Regent's Park
London
NW1 6AS
Tel: 0171 616 6629
e-mail: central@aims.co.uk
Web site: www.aims.co.uk
Contact: Louise Berwin

Business description: Accountants for business
BFA membership: No
No. of franchise outlets: 36
Year business started: 1992

Start-up capital (minimum): To cover office equipment
Initial fee: Minimum of £750 to maximum of £5,650
Management fee: On a sliding scale, 12.5% down to 6.25%
Proportion of start-up capital that can be arranged: Dependent on
individual circumstances

Alphagraphics
Thornburgh Road
Eastfield
Scarborough
North Yorkshire
YO11 3UY
Tel: 01723 502222
e-mail: a.dalton@alphagraphics.co.uk
Web site: www.alphagraphics.co.uk
Contact: Andrew Dalton

Business description: Design, copy, print franchise
BFA membership: Full
No. of franchise outlets: 14
Year business started: 1988

Start-up capital (minimum): £50,000
Initial fee: £24,000
Management fee: Royalties on sales, sliding scale 10%, 7%, 5%
Proportion of start-up capital that can be arranged: Up to 50%

Amtrak Express Parcels Ltd
Company House
Tower Hill
Bristol
BS2 0AZ
Tel: 0990 456456
e-mail: marketing@amtrak.co.uk
Web site: http://www.amtrak.co.uk
Contact: Franchise Manager

Business description: Overnight and international parcel company
BFA membership: Full
No. of franchise outlets: 340
Year business started: 1987

Start-up capital (minimum): £19,000 (to include working capital)
Initial fee: £12,500 (usually)
Management fee: Nil
Proportion of start-up capital that can be arranged: 60%

Apache
Apache House
La Route de St Aubin
St Helier
Jersey
Channel Islands
JE2 3SG
Tel: 01534 629300
Fax: 01534 607029
e-mail: n/a
Web site: n/a
Contact: Rodney J Ison (Managing Director)

Business description: Tourist guides
BFA membership: Provisional
No. of franchise outlets: 7 (and 5 pending)
Year business started: Parent company 1992, Apache Franchising 1997

Start-up capital (minimum): £3,000–£5,000
Initial fee: £10,000
Management fee: 10% of turnover, 0.5% advertising budget
Proportion of start-up capital that can be arranged: 66% of initial fee
and start-up capital

Apollo Blinds
Cold Hesledon Industrial Estate
Seaham
SR7 8ST
Tel: 0191 513 0061
e-mail: n/a
Web site: http://www.lds.co.uk/franchise/apollo
Contact: Graham Mylchreest

Business description: Window furnishings retailer
BFA membership: Full
No. of franchise outlets: 58
Year business started: 1970

Start-up capital (minimum): £15,000
Initial fee: £9,999
Management fee: Nil
Proportion of start-up capital that can be arranged: 70%

Aquaid Franchising Ltd
51 Newnham Road
Cambridge
CB3 9EY
Tel: 01223 508109
e-mail: n/a
Web site: www.aquaid.co.uk
Contact: Paul Searle

Business description: Providing water coolers and water to businesses
BFA membership: Provisional
No. of franchise outlets: 7
Year business started: 1999

Start-up capital (minimum): £50,000
Initial fee: £8,000
Management fee: 10%
Proportion of start-up capital that can be arranged: 60%

Art 4 Fun Ltd
444 Chiswick High Road
London
W4 5TT
Tel: 0181 994 4800
e-mail: paint@art4fun.com
Web site: www.art4fun.com
Contact: David Berger

Business description: Retail outlet for customers to paint ceramics, wood, glass, silk, etc
BFA membership: Applied for
No. of franchise outlets: Nil
Year business started: 1997

Start-up capital (minimum): £60,000
Initial fee: £12,000 (included in above £60,000)
Management fee: 4% plus 4% marketing fee
Proportion of start-up capital that can be arranged: Nil

ASC Partnership plc
3 Park Road
Regent's Park
London
NW1 6AS
Tel: 0171 616 6628
e-mail: central@asc.co.uk
Web site: www.asc.co.uk
Contact: Louise Berwin

Business description: Finance for business
BFA membership: No
No. of franchise outlets: 30
Year business started: 1969

Start-up capital (minimum): £10,000 to cover office equipment
Initial fee: £7,500 minimum to £47,500 maximum
Management fee: On a sliding scale, 15% down to 7.5%
Proportion of start-up capital that can be arranged: Dependent on
individual circumstances

Blazes Fireplace Centres plc
Pendle House
Phoenix Way
Burnley
BB11 5SX
Tel: 01282 831176
e-mail: info@blazes.co.uk
Web site: www.blazes.co.uk
Contact: Michael Eyre

Business description: Fireplace retailers
BFA membership: Associate
No. of franchise outlets: 31
Year business started: 1989

Start-up capital (minimum): £15,000 cash input – £35,000 total
Initial fee: £8,000
Management fee: 8% net sales
Proportion of start-up capital that can be arranged: 70%

Body Reform
Western Avenue
Bridgend Industrial Estate
Bridgend
CF31 3RT
Tel: 01656 766566
e-mail: sales@body-reform.co.uk
Web site: www.body-reform.co.uk
Contact: Mrs D Bushell

Business description: Manufacturer and retailer of cosmetics and
toiletries
BFA membership: No
No. of franchise outlets: Nil in UK. Company operates overseas on a
Master Licence basis – represented in 20 countries world-wide
Year business started: 1985

Start-up capital (minimum): £40–50,000 depending on location
Initial fee: Single shop franchise £15,000
Management fee: Nil
Proportion of start-up capital that can be arranged: Client responsibility

Bond-a-Frame Ltd
15a St Pancras
Chichester
West Sussex
PO19 1SJ
Tel: 01243 789343
Fax: 01243 786345
e-mail: n/a
Web site: www.bondaframe@townchoice.co.uk
Contact: Mike Bond

Business description: DIY and custom picture framing
BFA membership: No
No. of franchise outlets: 1
Year business started: 1984 (franchise 1997)

Start-up capital (minimum): £35,000
Initial fee: £3,000
Management fee: 10% (marketing fee 2.5%)
Proportion of start-up capital that can be arranged: 40%

Bounders Bruncherie Ltd
Unit 6, Barnwell Business Park
Barnwell Drive
Cambridge
CB5 8UX
Tel: 01223 518866
e-mail: n/a
Web site: n/a
Contact: Karen Riley

Business description: Sandwich bar/café
BFA membership: Provisional
No. of franchise outlets: 4
Year business started: 1997

Start-up capital (minimum): £75,000
Initial fee: £10,000
Management fee: 7%
Proportion of start-up capital that can be arranged: 70%

BTA (UK) Ltd (T A Computa Tune)
Oxford Street
Accrington
BB5 1QX
Tel: 01254 355600
e-mail: n/a
Web site: n/a
Contact: Mr A Whittaker

Business description: Mobile vehicle services
BFA membership: Full
No. of franchise outlets: Nil
Year business started: 1981 (franchised 1985)

Start-up capital (minimum): £14,000
Initial fee: £3,000
Management fee: 9%
Proportion of start-up capital that can be arranged: Nil

BTC
BTC House
Unit 4, Humber Trading Estate
Humber Road
London
NW2 6DW
Tel: 0181 208 1155
e-mail: info@britishtshirt.co.uk
Web site: www.britishtshirt.co.uk
Contact: Glenn Hyams

Business description: Wholesalers of promotional clothing
BFA membership: No
No. of franchise outlets: 4
Year business started: 1989

Start-up capital (minimum): £50,000
Initial fee: £10,000
Management fee: Nil
Proportion of start-up capital that can be arranged: Nil

Business Post Ltd
Wolseley Drive
Heartlands
Birmingham
B8 2SQ
Tel: 0121 335 1115
e-mail: michelle_recardo@business-post.com
Web site: n/a
Contact: Michelle Recardo

Business description: UK & world-wide delivery of mail and parcels
BFA membership: No
No. of franchise outlets: 41
Year business started: 1971

Start-up capital (minimum): £100,000–£250,000
Initial fee: £15,000 plus VAT and business base fee
Management fee: £100,000–£250,000
Proportion of start-up capital that can be arranged: Negotiable with an approved bank

Additional information: Business Post is one of the largest independent UK parcel and express mail delivery companies, delivering throughout the UK and world-wide. We operate through a nation-wide network of over 60 locations.

Card Connection Ltd
Park House
South Street
Farnham
GU9 7QQ
Tel: 01252 892300
e-mail: ho@card-connection.co.uk
Web site: n/a
Contact: Tony Winchester

Business description: Distribution of greeting cards
BFA membership: Full
No. of franchise outlets: 80
Year business started: 1992

Start-up capital (minimum): £25,000
Initial fee: £15,000
Management fee: Nil
Proportion of start-up capital that can be arranged: Nil

Cash Generator Ltd
113 Bradshawgate
Bolton
BL1 1QD
Tel: 01204 371871
e-mail: info@cash.generator.thruthe.net
Web site: http://www.cash.generator.thruthe.net
Contact: Brian Lewis

Business description: Cash Generator buys goods from the public for
instant cash, sells pre-used items and discounted new products with no
quibble guarantees, and offers instant cash raising and cheque cashing
services.
BFA membership: No
No. of franchise outlets: 22
Year business started: 1994

Start-up capital (minimum): £85,000
Initial fee: £7,950
Management fee: 5.5% of turnover
Proportion of start-up capital that can be arranged: Nil

Catermat Ltd
13 Redhills Road
South Woodham Ferrars
Chelmsford
CM3 5UJ
Tel: 01245 322465
e-mail: sales@catermat.co.uk
Web site: www.catermat.co.uk
Contact: Derek Pritchard

Business description: Coffee and vending
BFA membership: No
No. of franchise outlets: 10
Year business started: 1970

Start-up capital (minimum): £9,750
Initial fee: £9,750
Management fee: Nil
Proportion of start-up capital that can be arranged: Nil

Chem-Dry Northern & Southern Ltd
Colonial House, Swinemoor Lane
Beverley
East Riding of Yorkshire HU17 0LS
Tel: 01482 872770
e-mail: n/a
Web site: n/a
Contact: Brian Lockie (Senior Business Development Manager)

Business description: A worldwide franchise company offering a
proven, successful business formula using uniquely patented systems
and solutions, serving the domestic, commercial and insurance carpet
and upholstery cleaning sector
BFA membership: Full
No. of franchise outlets: 523 (nation-wide)
Year business started: 1987

Start-up capital (minimum): £17,950 plus VAT
Initial fee: £8,000
Management fee: £154.57 per month
Proportion of start-up capital that can be arranged: 70%

Chemical Express
Spring Road, Smethwick
West Midlands B66 1PT
Tel: 0121 525 4040
e-mail: n/a
Web site: n/a
Contact: Les Gray

Business description: Mobile supply of hygiene and cleaning products to industry
BFA membership: Full
No. of franchise outlets: 104
Year business started: 1985

Start-up capital (minimum): £16,900
Initial fee: £7,000
Management fee: 7.5%
Proportion of start-up capital that can be arranged: 80%

CICO Chimney Linings Ltd
Westleton
Saxmundham
Suffolk
IP17 3EF
Tel: 01728 648608
e-mail: n/a
Web site: n/a
Contact: R J Hadfield

Business description: Lining of domestic and non-domestic chimneys
BFA membership: No
No. of franchise outlets: 20
Year business started: 1982

Start-up capital (minimum): £21,000
Initial fee: £8,000
Management fee: 7.5%
Proportion of start-up capital that can be arranged: Nil

Colneis Marketing Ltd
York House
2–4 York Road
Felixstowe
IP11 7QQ
Tel: 01394 271668
e-mail: n/a
Web site: n/a
Contact: John Botting

Business description: Greeting cards
BFA membership: Provisional
No. of franchise outlets: 37
Year business started: 1994

Start-up capital (minimum): £5,000
Initial fee: £275–£575
Management fee: Nil
Proportion of start-up capital that can be arranged: Variable

Copleys Franchising Ltd
22 The Pavement
York
YO1 2ND
Tel: 01904 624880
e-mail: n/a
Web site: n/a
Contact: Hannah Broadley

Business description: Property management
BFA membership: No
No. of franchise outlets: 18
Year business started: 1993

Start-up capital (minimum): £7,500
Initial fee: £2,750
Management fee: 7.5% gross takings
Proportion of start-up capital that can be arranged: Nil

Countrywide Grounds Maintenance
Teejay Court
Alderley Road
Wilmslow
SK9 1NT
Tel: 01625 529000
e-mail: franchise@countrywidegrounds.co.uk
Web site: n/a
Contact: Simon Stott

Business description: National grounds maintenance contractors
BFA membership: No
No. of franchise outlets: 51
Year business started: 1986

Start-up capital (minimum): £20,000
Initial fee: £27,750 (franchise cost)
Management fee: Royalty – 10%
Proportion of start-up capital that can be arranged: To be discussed

County Homesearch International plc
The Sight Centre
Newham Quay
Truro
TR1 2DP
Tel: 01872 223349
e-mail: headoffice@county-homesearch.co.uk
Web site: www.county-homesearch.co.uk
Contact: Jonathan A Haward

Business description: Providers of a bespoke home finding service
BFA membership: No
No. of franchise outlets: 25
Year business started: 1991

Start-up capital (minimum): £25,000
Initial fee: £15,000
Management fee: 7.5%
Proportion of start-up capital that can be arranged: By arrangement

Decorating Den
Bowditch, Membury
Axminster, Devon, EX13 7TY
Tel: 01404 881789
e-mail: decden@eclipse.co.uk
Web site: decoratingden.co.uk (under construction)
Contact: –

Business description: Mobile interior design and supply
BFA membership: IFA membership
No. of franchise outlets: Nil
Year business started: USA – 1970, UK – 1989

Start-up capital (minimum): Nil
Initial fee: Nil
Management fee: 11.7%
Proportion of start-up capital that can be arranged: Nil

Dixy Fried Chickens Euro Ltd
185 Town Road
Edmonton
London
N9 0HL
Tel: 0181 345 6675
e-mail: n/a
Web site: n/a
Contact: A Mattmood

Business description: Fast food take-away/restaurant
BFA membership: No
No. of franchise outlets: 32
Year business started: 1986

Start-up capital (minimum): £70,000
Initial fee: £5,000
Management fee: 4% turnover
Proportion of start-up capital that can be arranged: £35,000 subject to status

Dor-2-Dor
Clare Lodge
41 Holly Bush Lane
Harpenden
AL5 4AY
Tel: 01582 462744
e-mail: dor2dor@val-u-pak.com
Web site: n/a
Contact: Jeff Frankling

Business description: Door-to-door leaflet distribution
BFA membership: No
No. of franchise outlets: 35
Year business started: 1994

Start-up capital (minimum): £1,500
Initial fee: £1,500
Management fee: 10% (£35 monthly minimum)
Proportion of start-up capital that can be arranged: Nil

The Dorber Collection Ltd
6 Grosvenor Road
Paignton
TQ4 5AY
Tel: 01803 529539
e-mail: dorber.couk@virgin.net
Web site: dorber.home.ml.org
Contact: John Richardson, Robin Richardson

Business description: Greeting card franchise
BFA membership: No
No. of franchise outlets: 10
Year business started: 1994

Start-up capital (minimum): £12,850
Initial fee: As above
Management fee: Nil
Proportion of start-up capital that can be arranged: Nil

Dreams plc
Knaves Beech
High Wycombe
Buckinghamshire
HP10 9QY
Tel: 01628 535353
e-mail: beds@dreams.plc.uk
Web site: www.dreams.plc.uk
Contact: Larry Dyer

Business description: Bed retailer
BFA membership: No
No. of franchise outlets: 5
Year business started: 1985

Start-up capital (minimum): Negotiable
Initial fee: Negotiable
Management fee: Negotiable
Proportion of start-up capital that can be arranged: Negotiable

Drinkmaster Ltd
Plymouth Road
Liskeard
PL14 3PG
Tel: 01579 342082
e-mail: n/a
Web site: www.drinkmaster.com/drinkmaster
Contact: Margaret Bunton

Business description: Drinks and vending systems
BFA membership: Associate
No. of franchise outlets: 45
Year business started: Company established 1962 (franchise established 1995)

Start-up capital (minimum): £10,500
Initial fee: £7,000
Management fee: TBA
Proportion of start-up capital that can be arranged: Nil

Driver Hire Group Services Ltd
Progress House
Castlefields Lane
Bingley
BD16 2AB
Tel: 01274 551166
e-mail: info@driver-hire.co.uk
Web site: www.driver-hire.co.uk
Contact: Alan Cawthorne

Business description: Specialist employment agency (drivers)
BFA membership: Full
No. of franchise outlets: 78
Year business started: 1983

Start-up capital (minimum): £25,000 plus working capital
Initial fee: £15,000
Management fee: 5% Management, 2% Administration, 1% Advertising
Proportion of start-up capital that can be arranged: Up to 50%

Additional information: 1998 saw price adjustment to make this an even more affordable opportunity. A special lease package for equipment is arranged by the franchisor and now has added benefit of unique training facility.

Duds 'n' Suds (UK) Ltd
141 Strand Road
Derry
Northern Ireland
BT48 7PB
Tel: 01504 262615
e-mail: info@dudsnsuds.iol.ie
web site: n/a
Contact: Damian Nicell

Business description: Laundry and dry clean franchise
BFA membership: No
No. of franchise outlets: 7
Year business started: 1992

Start-up capital (minimum): Personal – £35,000
Total – £90,000
Initial fee: £15,000
Management fee: 5%
Proportion of start-up capital that can be arranged: Nil

Durham Pine Ltd
Colima Avenue
Hylton Riverside
Sunderland
Tyne & Wear
SR5 3XF
Tel: 0191 516 9300
e-mail: n/a
Web site: n/a
Contact: Rita Ferenson

Business description: Pine furniture retailer
BFA membership: Full
No. of franchise outlets: 37
Year business started: 1986

Start-up capital (minimum): £45,000
Initial fee: £10,000
Management fee: 5% of monthly bankings
Proportion of start-up capital that can be arranged: Up to 50% from
leading banks

Fast Food Systems Ltd (T A Southern Fried Chicken)
Unit 1
Headley Park 9
Headley Road East
Woodley
Reading
RG5 4SQ
Tel: 01189 441100
e-mail: sales@fast-food-system.co.uk
Web site: www.southern-fried-chicken.com
Contact: A J Withers

Business description: Fried chicken
BFA membership: No
No. of franchise outlets: 650
Year business started: 1980

Start-up capital (minimum): £65,000
Initial fee: Nil
Management fee: Nil
Proportion of start-up capital that can be arranged: 70%

First Impressions
The Coach House
Ramsey Manor
High Street
Burwell
Cambridge
CB5 0HD
Tel: 01638 741166
e-mail: ph@firstimpressions.demon.co.uk
Web site: Under development
Contact: Patrick Halpin

Business description: Personal & corporate image consultancy
BFA membership: No
No. of franchise outlets: 200 worldwide
Year business started: 1984

Start-up capital (minimum): £4,000
Initial fee: £3,100
Management fee: Nil
Proportion of start-up capital that can be arranged: Nil

Fix-a-Chip Ltd
The Car Smart Centre
Vermont
Washington
Tyne & Wear
NE37 2AX
Tel: 0191 417 0577
e-mail: n/a
Web site: http://www.lds.co.uk/franchise/fixachip
Contact: Bryan Stapley

Business description: Mobile minor vehicle repairs
BFA membership: Provisional
No. of franchise outlets: 36
Year business started: 1995

Start-up capital (minimum): £6,000
Initial fee: £15,000
Management fee: 10%
Proportion of start-up capital that can be arranged: 50%

The Flat Roof Company
Unit 7C, Guardian Park
Station Industrial Estate
Tadcaster
North Yorkshire
LS24 9SG
Tel: 0800 212 548
e-mail: flatroofco@compuserve.com
Web site: n/a
Contact: Kevin Moody, Richard Wolfenden

Business description: High performance flat roof contractors
BFA membership: Associate
No. of franchise outlets: 21
Year business started: 1987 (franchised 1993)

Start-up capital (minimum): £17,500 plus VAT
Initial fee: £2,500
Management fee: 10%
Proportion of start-up capital that can be arranged: 50%–70% subject to status

Focus Micro Systems
Sherlock House
Bayswater Farm Road
Headington
Oxford
OX3 8BX
Tel: 01865 766241
e-mail: n/a
Web site: n/a
Contact: Mr Duncan Samuel

Business description: Computer software and systems house
BFA membership: No
No. of franchise outlets: 1
Year business started: 1981

Start-up capital (minimum): £10,000
Initial fee: £10,000
Management fee: 10%
Proportion of start-up capital that can be arranged: Nil

Additional information: Focus is a provider of specialist software into
particular vertical markets. We have had particular success in the
property section, with over 1,000 clients in that area.

The Food Weighouse Ltd
4 Walkerville Industrial Park
Catterick
North Yorkshire
DL9 4SA
Tel: 01748 834646
e-mail: n/a
Web site: n/a
Contact: Richard Russell

Business description: Loose food retailing
BFA membership: No
No. of franchise outlets: 31 plus 23 company shops
Year business started: 1988

Start-up capital (minimum): £35,000
Initial fee: £3,000
Management fee: Nil
Proportion of start-up capital that can be arranged: Nil

Furniture Medic
Service Master House
Leicester Road
Anstey
Leicestershire
LE7 7AT
Tel: 0116 236 4646
e-mail: n/a
Web site: n/a
Contact: Eric Sturdy

Business description: On-site furniture restoration
BFA membership: Full (listed as Service Master)
No. of franchise outlets: 48
Year business started: 1997

Start-up capital (minimum): £6,000+
Initial fee: £9,500
Management fee: 10%
Proportion of start-up capital that can be arranged: 70%

The Garage Door Company (Scotland) Ltd
Unit 7
Russell Road Industrial Estate
Russell Road
Edinburgh
EH11 2NN
Tel: 0131 337 3332
e-mail: sales@garage-door.co.uk
Web site: http://www.garage-door.co.uk
Contact: Allan Macreath

Business description: Installation, supply and repair of doors, gates, operators
BFA membership: No
No. of franchise outlets: 9
Year business started: 1977

Start-up capital (minimum): £19,500
Initial fee: £500
Management fee: 6% of sales
Proportion of start-up capital that can be arranged: Personal to applicants

The Great Escape
47 Burns Statue Square
Ayr
Scotland
KA7 1SZ
Tel: 01292 610600
e-mail: directors@thegreatescape.co.uk
Web site: www.thegreatescape.co.uk
Contact: James M Fraser

Business description: Walk in retail – outdoor leisure
BFA membership: No
No. of franchise outlets: 2
Year business started: 1950

Start-up capital (minimum): £60,000 (50% financed)
Initial fee: £5,000
Management fee: 7% of sales
Proportion of start-up capital that can be arranged: 50–60%

Greenalls Inn Partnership
PO Box 2
Greenalls Avenue
Warrington
Cheshire
WA4 6RH
Tel: 01925 651234
e-mail: john.wilkin@greenalls.com
Web site: www.greenalls-franchise.co.uk
Contact: John Wilkin

Business description: Pub franchising
BFA membership: Full
No. of franchise outlets: 960
Year business started: 1990

Start-up capital (minimum): £23,000
Initial fee: From £4,000
Management fee: From 2% of turnover
Proportion of start-up capital that can be arranged: 50%

Greencare Ltd
Greencare House
Sharpness
Gloucestershire
GL13 9UD
Tel: 01453 511366
e-mail: sales@greencare.co.uk
Web site: www.greencare.co.uk
Contact: Malcolm Macleod, Mrs Rebecca Lee

Business description: Recycling service provider to businesses
BFA membership: No
No. of franchise outlets: 25
Year business started: 1993

Start-up capital (minimum): £24,000
Initial fee: £10,000
Management fee: Nil
Proportion of start-up capital that can be arranged: Nil

Additional information: Franchise page on our web site, together with up-to-date product/service information: www.greencare.co.uk

Greenrose Network incorporating Country Properties
The Old Limes
41 High Street
Baldock
Hertfordshire
SG7 6BG
Tel: 01462 896148
e-mail: n/a
Web site: n/a
Contact: Michael Rogers

Business description: Estate agency franchise
BFA membership: No
No. of franchise outlets: 18
Year business started: 1974

Start-up capital (minimum): £15,000
Initial fee: £3,000
Management fee: 6.5% of gross turnover
Proportion of start-up capital that can be arranged: Two thirds

Additional information: Progressive residential estate agency business. New system just introduced enabling people with business but not estate agency experience to run the business with equal chance of success.

Guardsman-Safeclean
152 Milton Park
Abingdon
Oxfordshire
OX14 4SD
Tel: 01235 444757
e-mail: n/a
Web site: n/a
Contact: Hilary Reynolds

Business description: Furnishing care experts
BFA membership: Full
No. of franchise outlets: 68
Year business started: 1971

Start-up capital (minimum): £18,000
Initial fee: £15,950 plus VAT
Management fee: 10%
Proportion of start-up capital that can be arranged: 70%

Additional information: Operating at the upper end of the domestic
market-place with high repeat and referral business, franchisees enjoy
working from home with a van-based operation providing expert
furnishing care.

The Handwash Ltd
755 Ashton Old Road
Manchester
M11 2HB
Tel: 0161 231 0900
e-mail: n/a
Web site: n/a
Contact: Nigel White

Business description: Hand car wash
BFA membership: Provisional
No. of franchise outlets: 5
Year business started: 1992

Start-up capital (minimum): £60,000
Initial fee: £7,500
Management fee: 10%
Proportion of start-up capital that can be arranged: £40,000

The Historical Research Centre
22 King Street
Knutsford
WA16 6DL
Tel: 01565 631911
Fax: 01565 631922
e-mail: n/a
Web site: n/a
Contact: G Fluebster

Business description: Franchisor of heraldic giftware produced at point of sale
BFA membership: No
No. of franchise outlets: 15
Year business started: UK – 1995

Start-up capital (minimum): £2,000
Initial fee: £350
Management fee: Nil
Proportion of start-up capital that can be arranged: Nil

Home Ice Products Ltd
Unit 4
Norgate Terrace
Northern Road Industrial Estate
Newark
Nottinghamshire
NG24 2EW
Tel: 01636 612500
e-mail: hemglas@vnetuk.com.
Web site: www.vnetuk.com\hemglas
Contact: J Rudd

Business description: Frozen food distributors
BFA membership: No
No. of franchise outlets: 15
Year business started: 1992

Start-up capital (minimum): £3,000
Initial fee: £500
Management fee: £1,800 p.a.
Proportion of start-up capital that can be arranged: Nil

Initial City Link Ltd
Kempton House, Batavia Road
Sunbury-on-Thames
Middlesex
TW16 5LR
Tel: 01932 788799
e-mail: n/a
Web site: www.city-link.co.uk
Contact: Michael Cooke (Managing Director)

Business description: Parcel delivery
BFA membership: Full
No. of franchise outlets: 70
Year business started: 1969

Start-up capital (minimum): £20,000
Initial fee: Variable
Management fee: 10%
Proportion of start-up capital that can be arranged: Nil

Intoto Kitchens
Shaw Cross Court
Shaw Cross Business Park
Dewsbury
WF12 7RF
Tel: 01924 487900
e-mail: info@intoto.co.uk
Web site: www.intoto.co.uk
Contact: David Watts

Business description: Fitted kitchen retailer
BFA membership: Full
No. of franchise outlets: 30
Year business started: 1979

Start-up capital (minimum): £15,000
Initial fee: £5,000
Management fee: Nil
Proportion of start-up capital that can be arranged: 66%

Kall Kwik Printing (UK) Ltd
Kall Kwik House
106 Pembroke Road
Ruislip
Middlesex
HA4 8NW
Tel: 01895 872000
e-mail: franchise.sales@kallkwik.co.uk
Web site: www.kallkwik.co.uk
Contact: Ms Janet Twining

Business description: Print, copy and design
BFA membership: Full
No. of franchise outlets: 187
Year business started: 1978

Start-up capital (minimum): £135,000
Initial fee: £4,500
Management fee: 10%
Proportion of start-up capital that can be arranged: £90,000

Kendlebell Ltd
7th Floor
Carolyn House
22–26 Dingwall Road
Croydon
CR0 9XF
Tel: 0181 288 0617
e-mail: kendlebell@aol.com
Web site: n/a
Contact: Neil Peters

Business description: UK's no. 1 telephone answering franchise
BFA membership: Provisional
No. of franchise outlets: 8
Year business started: 1997

Start-up capital (minimum): £10,000
Initial fee: £10,000
Management fee: 10%
Proportion of start-up capital that can be arranged: 50% bank funding –
subject to status

Additional information: Kendlebell provides an excellent first
impression for professional small businesses by diverting incoming
calls. Our telephone answering service is reliable, friendly and efficient.
Comprehensive training, billings service and technical support.

Keytracker Franchising Ltd
Keyper House
19 Whitehall Road
Halesowen
B63 3JR
Tel: 0121 585 0123
e-mail: franchising@keytracker.com
Web site: www.keytracker.com
Contact: Steve Reed

Business description: Key, lock or valuable item tracking system
BFA membership: Application pending
No. of franchise outlets: 6
Year business started: 1997

Start-up capital (minimum): £12,000
Initial fee: £9,750
Management fee: Nil
Proportion of start-up capital that can be arranged: 50%

M&B Marquees Ltd
Premier House
Tennyson Drive
Pitsea
Basildon
Essex
SS13 3BT
Tel: 01268 558002
e-mail: sales@mbmarquees.prestel.co.uk
Web site: http://www.mb_marquees.com
Contact: John Mansfield

Business description: Marquee and equipment hire
BFA membership: No
No. of franchise outlets: 12
Year business started: 1977

Start-up capital (minimum): £35,000
Initial fee: £3,000
Management fee: £250 monthly
Proportion of start-up capital that can be arranged: £10,000

Martin & Co.
6–8 Union Street
Yeovil
BA20 1PQ
Tel: 01935 426000
e-mail: head.office@martinco.com
Web site: www.martinco.com
Contact: Tim Rose (National Franchising Director)

Business description: Residential lettings and management
BFA membership: Associate
No. of franchise outlets: 21
Year business started: 1986

Start-up capital (minimum): Variable
Initial fee: £6,900 plus VAT
Management fee: 9% of gross income
Proportion of start-up capital that can be arranged: 70%

Master Thatchers Ltd
Faircross Offices
Stratfield Saye
Reading
Berkshire
RG7 2BT
Tel: 01256 880828
e-mail: n/a
Web site: n/a
Contact: R West

Business description: Roof thatching
BFA membership: Full
No. of franchise outlets: 22
Year business started: 1983

Start-up capital (minimum): £30,000
Initial fee: £25,000
Management fee: 5%–10% of turnover
Proportion of start-up capital that can be arranged: Nil

Additional information: Wholly owned subsidiary of the National Farmers' Union Mutual, the tenth largest insurance group in the UK. Franchisees have won Thatched House of the Year Competition.

McDonald's Restaurants Ltd
11–59 High Road
East Finchley
London
N2 8AW
Tel: 0181 700 7154
e-mail: n/a
Web site: n/a
Contact: Krissy Elliott, Derrick Smith

Business description: Quick service restaurant
BFA membership: Full
No. of franchise outlets: 245
Year business started: 1974

Start-up capital (minimum): £35,000
Initial fee: £30,000
Management fee: Nil
Proportion of start-up capital that can be arranged: Nil

Metro-Rod plc
Metro House
Churchill Way
Macclesfield
Cheshire
SK11 6AY
Tel: 01625 869525
e-mail: wendy.ayres@thameswater.co.uk
Web site: n/a
Contact: Charles Sindall

Business description: Drain care and repair
BFA membership: Full
No. of franchise outlets: 40
Year business started: 1983

Start-up capital (minimum): £45,000
Initial fee: £15,000
Management fee: 25%
Proportion of start-up capital that can be arranged: 70%

Mixamate Concrete
11 Westdown
Great Bookham
Surrey
KT23 4LJ
Tel: 01372 456714
e-mail: n/a
Web site: n/a
Contact: Mr Peter Slinn

Business description: Concrete delivery service
BFA membership: No (Full member retired)
No. of franchise outlets: 27
Year business started: 1978

Start-up capital (minimum): From £21,000
Initial fee: From £5,000
Management fee: 6%
Proportion of start-up capital that can be arranged: 70%

Mr Cod Ltd
6–7 High Street
Woking Surrey
GU21 1BG
Tel: 01483 755407
e-mail: n/a
Web site: n/a
Contact: Mr J A Brewer

Business description: Fast food fish and chicken
BFA membership: No
No. of franchise outlets: 8
Year business started: 1980

Start-up capital (minimum): £35,000–£75,000
Initial fee: Variable
Management fee: Variable
Proportion of start-up capital that can be arranged: Nil

Additional information: Fast food take-away or restaurant selling
quality English fish and chips and American fried chicken.

The Natural Way Franchising
Dartmouth House
Westlands
Newcastle under Lyme
Staffordshire
ST5 3PA
Tel: 01782 711122/766766/719019
e-mail: n/a
Web site: dietandweightloss.com
Contact: Mr Peter Bell-Langford

Business description: Weight loss consultancy
BFA membership: Accepted as affiliate member but cancelled by
company
No. of franchise outlets: 26
Year business started: 1993

Start-up capital (minimum): £3,500
Initial fee: Nil – free franchise
Management fee: Nil
Proportion of start-up capital that can be arranged: Nil

Neal's Yard (Natural Remedies) Ltd
26–34 Ingate Place
London
SW8 3NS
Tel: 0171 498 1686
e-mail: mail@nealsyardremedies.com
Web site: From Summer 1999
Contact: Romy Fraser

Business description: Natural medicines and toiletries
BFA membership: Full
No. of franchise outlets: 10
Year business started: 1981

Start-up capital (minimum): £85,000
Initial fee: £12,500
Management fee: Annual 5%
Proportion of start-up capital that can be arranged: Nil

Nectar Manufacturing Ltd
1 Meadowbank Road
Carrickfergus
Co. Antrim
BT38 8XX
Tel: 01960 351580
e-mail: info@nectar.eunet.co.uk
Web site: http://www.nectar-cosmetics.com
Contact: Mr R B Waring

Business description: Manufacturer of beauty products
BFA membership: No
No. of franchise outlets: 280
Year business started: 1984

Start-up capital (minimum): £50,000
Initial fee: £10,000 minimum
Management fee: Nil
Proportion of start-up capital that can be arranged: Nil

Nevada Bob UK Ltd
The Rotunda
Broadgate Circle
London
EC2M 2BN
Tel: 0171 628 4999
e-mail: mitch@nevadabob.co.uk
Web site: n/a
Contact: Mr Phil Smith

Business description: Golf retail
BFA membership: No
No. of franchise outlets: 39
Year business started: 1990

Start-up capital (minimum): £160,000
Initial fee: £47,500
Management fee: 3% royalty
Proportion of start-up capital that can be arranged: Two thirds (subject to status)

Nippers UK Franchising Ltd
Mansers
Nizels Lane
Hildenborough
Kent
TN11 8NX
Tel: 01732 838333
e-mail: nippers@dircon.co.uk
Web site: n/a
Contact: Mrs S G Cassel (Managing Director)

Business description: Retail – nursery goods and toys
BFA membership: Associate
No. of franchise outlets: 8
Year business started: 1991

Start-up capital (minimum): TBA, details on application
Initial fee: TBA, details on application
Management fee: TBA, details on application
Proportion of start-up capital that can be arranged: TBA, details on application

O'Brien's Irish Sandwich Bars
24 South Williams Street
Dublin 2
Ireland
Tel: 00 353 1 671 5176
e-mail: e-mail-brody@iol.ie
Web site: www.obriens.ie
Contact: Olive Hipwell

Business description: Upmarket sandwich bars
BFA membership: Associate
No. of franchise outlets: 35
Year business started: 1988

Start-up capital (minimum): £40,000–£100,000
Initial fee: £9,000 plus VAT
Management fee: 6% of net turnover
Proportion of start-up capital that can be arranged: 50%

Ordning & Reda
22 New Row
London
WC2N 4LA
Tel: 0171 240 8090
e-mail: n/a
Web site: n/a
Contact: Mr Gustaf Frithz

Business description: Retail – designed paper products
BFA membership: No
No. of franchise outlets: 40
Year business started: 1982

Start-up capital (minimum): £100,000
Initial fee: Nil
Management fee: 8%
Proportion of start-up capital that can be arranged: Nil

Oscar Pet Foods
Bannister Hall Mill
Higher Walton
Preston
PR5 4DB
Tel: 01772 626789
e-mail: discover@oscars.co.uk
Web site: www.oscars.co.uk
Contact: Martin Dancy, Janet Walmsley

Business description: Pet food delivery and pet care service
BFA membership: Associate
No. of franchise outlets: 140
Year business started: 1990

Start-up capital (minimum): £4,000–£8,000
Initial fee: £6,000–£15,000
Management fee: £75 per month
Proportion of start-up capital that can be arranged: 50% subject to status

Paint Magic
79 Shepperton Road
London
N1 3DF
Tel: 0171 354 9696
e-mail: n/a
Web site: n/a
Contact: Sarah Delafield Cook

Business description: Retailer in decorative paints
BFA membership: Associate
No. of franchise outlets: 13
Year business started: 1993

Start-up capital (minimum): £40,000
Initial fee: £12,000
Management fee: Nil
Proportion of start-up capital that can be arranged: Nil

Paint Technik Ltd
PO Box 5066
Leighton Buzzard
LU7 7YS
Tel: 0800 298 5455
e-mail: painttechnik@dial.pipex.com
Web site: http://dspace.dial.pipex.com/town/place/rceio
Contact: Stephen Wood

Business description: Mobile automotive refinishing, smart repairs
BFA membership: Provisional
No. of franchise outlets: 90
Year business started: 1990

Start-up capital (minimum): £20,000
Initial fee: £14,995
Management fee: £1,000 p.a.
Proportion of start-up capital that can be arranged: 70%

PDC Copyprint
1 Church Lane
East Grinstead
West Sussex
RH19 3AZ
Tel: 01342 315321
e-mail: pdc@pdc-intl.demon.co.uk
Web site: www.pdccopyprint.co.uk
Contact: Stephen Ricketts

Business description: High street business printers (print, design, copying)
BFA membership: Full
No. of franchise outlets: 35
Year business started: 1982

Start-up capital (minimum): £37,000 (total £111,000)
Initial fee: £7,500
Management fee: 10% reducing to 5%
Proportion of start-up capital that can be arranged: Two thirds

Perfect Pizza
Perfect Pizza House
The Forum
Hanworth Lane
Chertsey
Surrey
KT16 9JX
Tel: 01932 568000
Fax: 01932 570628
e-mail: martin_clayton@perfectpizza.co.uk
Web site: n/a
Contact: –

Business description: Fast food pizza delivery and take-away
BFA membership: Full
No. of franchise outlets: 180
Year business started: 1978

Start-up capital (minimum): £25,000–£30,000
Initial fee: £8,000
Management fee: 8% (including marketing)
Proportion of start-up capital that can be arranged: Two thirds of
project (£75,000) subject to status

Petit Delice
19a St John Hill
London
SW11 1TN
Tel: 0171 801 0666
e-mail: n/a
Web site: n/a
Contact: Jacques Lherbier

Business description: French bakery, patisserie, café français
BFA membership: Application pending
No. of franchise outlets: 15
Year business started: 1985

Start-up capital (minimum): Nil
Initial fee: £7,000
Management fee: 5%
Proportion of start-up capital that can be arranged: Nil

Additional information: Petit Delice is a French-style bakery/café
français serving authentic French bakery products such as croissants
and pains au chocolat, manufactured in France and baked on the
premises.

Pitman Training Group plc
Pitman House
Audby Lane
Wetherby
LS22 7FD
Tel: 01937 548500
e-mail: n/a
Web site: www.pitman-training.co.uk
Contact: Mr James O'Brien

Business description: Computer training and education training centres
BFA membership: Full
No. of franchise outlets: 80
Year business started: 1992

Start-up capital (minimum): £50,000
Initial fee: £25
Management fee: Nil
Proportion of start-up capital that can be arranged: Nil

Practical Car & Van Rental
21–23 Little Broom Street
Camp Hill
Birmingham
B12 0EU
Tel: 0121 772 8599
Fax: 0121 766 6229
e-mail: n/a
Web site: www.practical.co.uk
Contact: Mr B Agnew

Business description: Car and van rental
BFA membership: Full
No. of franchise outlets: 190
Year business started: 1984

Start-up capital (minimum): £6,000
Initial fee: From £5,000
Management fee: TBA
Proportion of start-up capital that can be arranged: Nil

Priority Management
Oakwood
Spa Road
Melksham
Wiltshire
SN12 7TA
Tel: 01225 709533
e-mail: pmuk@prioritymanagement.com
Web site: www.prioritymanagement.com
Contact: Rachel Truelove

Business description: Training
BFA membership: Associate
No. of franchise outlets: 300 world-wide, 28 UK
Year business started: 1981

Start-up capital (minimum): £35,000
Initial fee: £35,000
Management fee: 9% plus 1% advertising levy
Proportion of start-up capital that can be arranged: Nil – franchisees
make own financing arrangements

Prontaprint Ltd
Axis 6
Rhodes Way
North Watford Industrial Estate
Watford
WD2 4YW
Tel: 01923 691400
e-mail: franchisesales@prontaprint.com
Web site: http://www.prontaprint.com
Contact: Julian Minwalla

Business description: Franchise, print, copy, design & communication services
BFA membership: Full
No. of franchise outlets: 245
Year business started: 1972

Start-up capital (minimum): £35,000 liquid
Initial fee: £12,500 plus VAT
Management fee: 10% of turnover
Proportion of start-up capital that can be arranged: Two thirds

Rainbow International
Spectrum House
Lower Oakham Way
Oakham Business Park
Mansfield
NG18 5BY
Tel: 01623 422488
e-mail: n/a
Web site: n/a
Contact: Ron Hutton

Business description: Carpet and upholstery cleaning
BFA membership: Full
No. of franchise outlets: 70
Year business started: UK 1988

Start-up capital (minimum): £10,000
Initial fee: £21,000
Management fee: 9% of gross turnover
Proportion of start-up capital that can be arranged: Nil

Additional information: Franchise is part of Dwyer Group, Texas.
Franchisor helping franchisees build business's national accounts,
including major insurance companies, use both as service providers.
Good expanding market, very profitable, suit managers.

Recognition Express Ltd
PO Box 7
Rugby Road
Hinckley
Leicestershire
LE10 2NE
Tel: 01455 232491
e-mail: post@recognition.co.uk
Web site: www.recognition-express.com
Contact: Ian Taylor

Business description: Business to business services
BFA membership: Full
No. of franchise outlets: 26
Year business started: 1979

Start-up capital (minimum): £50,000
Initial fee: £10,000
Management fee: 10%
Proportion of start-up capital that can be arranged: 70%

Ribbon Revival Ltd
Caslon Court
Pitronnerie Road
St Peter Port
Guernsey
Channel Islands
GY1 2RW
Tel: 01481 729552
e-mail: ribbonrev@post.guernsey.net
Web site: www.ribbonrevival.net
Contact: Mick Underdown

Business description: Desktop printers – sales, servicing, consumables
BFA membership: Associate
No. of franchise outlets: 45
Year business started: 1993

Start-up capital (minimum): £20,000
Initial fee: Varies with territory
Management fee: 9%
Proportion of start-up capital that can be arranged: Variable

Ripples Ltd
Chelsea House
London Road
Bath
BA1 6DB
Tel: 01225 447971
e-mail: n/a
Web site: n/a
Contact: Roger Kymo

Business description: Upmarket retail bathrooms
BFA membership: Provisional
No. of franchise outlets: 3
Year business started: 1988

Start-up capital (minimum): £15,000
Initial fee: £15,000
Management fee: 5%
Proportion of start-up capital that can be arranged: 50%

Additional information: Award-winning retail bathroom company.
Very upmarket showrooms in key locations selling top quality
European and English products.

Roaduser
Maccess
Spen Lane
Cleckheaton
West Yorkshire
BD19 4PG
Tel: 01274 870241
e-mail: n/a
Web site: n/a
Contact: Roy Rogers

Business description: Automotive retail franchise
BFA membership: Provisional
No. of franchise outlets: 5
Year business started: March 1998

Start-up capital (minimum): Initial investment from £750
Initial fee: See above
Management fee: See above
Proportion of start-up capital that can be arranged: £15,000

Additional information: RoadUser provides existing businesses, as well as those wishing to enter the parts and accessories car/leisure products retail sector, with the ability to capitalise on a proven formula. It includes signage, branded uniforms, stationery and local and national brand awareness programmes.

Rosemary Conley Diet & Fitness Clubs
Quorn House
Meeting Street
Quorn
Loughborough
Leicestershire
LE12 8EX
Tel: 01509 620222
e-mail: rcdfc@the-rosemary-conley-group.co.uk
Web site: http://www.the-rosemary-conley-group.co.uk
Contact: Simon Ford (General Manager)

Business description: Health and beauty
BFA membership: Associate
No. of franchise outlets: 175
Year business started: 1993

Start-up capital (minimum): Nil
Initial fee: £12,800
Management fee: £11 per class, per week
Proportion of start-up capital that can be arranged: Nil

Safeclean
152 Milton Park
Abingdon
Oxfordshire
OX14 4SD
Tel: 01235 833009
e-mail: n/a
Web site: n/a
Contact: Mr M Graham

Business description: Furnishing care specialists
BFA membership: Full
No. of franchise outlets: 70
Year business started: 1971

Start-up capital (minimum): £2,000–£3,000
Initial fee: £15,950 plus VAT
Management fee: 10% of turnover
Proportion of start-up capital that can be arranged: £10,000

Select Appointments
Ziggurat
Grosvenor Road
St Albans
AL1 3HW
Tel: 01727 790000
e-mail: l.ratcliffe@select.co.uk
Web site: n/a
Contact: Lorraine Ratcliffe

Business description: Recruitment services
BFA membership: Associate
No. of franchise outlets: 11
Year business started: 1980 (franchised 1994)

Start-up capital (minimum): £25,000 (total investment £90,000)
Initial fee: £12,500
Management fee: 7% of turnover
Proportion of start-up capital that can be arranged: Nil

Sevenoaks Sound & Vision
PO Box 496
Amersham
Buckinghamshire
HP7 0SA
Tel: 01494 431290
e-mail: n/a
Web site: http://www.lds.co.uk/franchise/sevenoaks-hifi
(Franchise enquiries to Amersham)

Head Office
109–113 London Road
Sevenoaks
Kent
TN13 1BH
Tel: 01732 741717
e-mail: n/a
Web site: http://www.lds.co.uk/franchise/sevenoaks-hifi
Contact: Malcolm Blockley

Business description: Specialist retailers of hi-fi, video, home cinema
BFA membership: Associate
No. of franchise outlets: 22
Year business started: 1972

Start-up capital (minimum): £75,000
Initial fee: £10,000
Management fee: 5% of turnover
Proportion of start-up capital that can be arranged: Two thirds

Additional information: Winners of the Sir Bernard Ingham Franchisor of the Year Award 1998.
Sites available in Liverpool, Manchester, Glasgow, Nottingham, Romford/Barkingside, Southend-on-Sea, Leicester, Wolverhampton, Huddersfield, Plymouth, Exeter.

Signs Express Ltd
The Old Church
St Matthew's Road
Norwich
NR1 1SP
Tel: 01603 625925
e-mail: fran@signsexpress.co.uk
Web site: signsexpress.co.uk
Contact: Jan Corbett

Business description: Sign services
BFA membership: Full
No. of franchise outlets: 65
Year business started: 1989

Start-up capital (minimum): Personal £27,500
Total £72,000
Initial fee: £16,500
Management fee: 7.5%
Proportion of start-up capital that can be arranged: 50%–70%

Snappy Snaps
10–12 Glenthorne Mews
Hammersmith
London
W6 0LJ
Tel: 0181 741 7474
e-mail: info@snappysnaps.co.uk
Web site: http://www.snappysnaps.co.uk
Contact: Hugh Jones

Business description: Photo processing
BFA membership: Full
No. of franchise outlets: 67
Year business started: 1983

Start-up capital (minimum): £30,000
Initial fee: £12,500
Management fee: 6%
Proportion of start-up capital that can be arranged: Nil

Stainbusters Ltd
15 Windmill Avenue
Woolpit Business Park
Bury St Edmunds
Suffolk
IP30 9UP
Tel: 0800 783 4721
e-mail: franchise@stainbusters.co.uk
Web site: www.stainbusters.com
Contact: Mrs Lorrie Finley

Business description: Carpet and furnishing dry cleaning
BFA membership: Associate
No. of franchise outlets: 37
Year business started: 1994

Start-up capital (minimum): £5,500
Initial fee: £9,950
Management fee: 10% (plus 2.5% advertising levy)
Proportion of start-up capital that can be arranged: 70%

Additional information: One of the fastest growing franchises in the
UK, Stainbusters provides the only guaranteed proven dry cleaning
service for carpets and furnishings. It offers investment opportunities at
area, district and regional level.

TaxAssist Direct Ltd
TaxAssist House
58 Thorpe Road
Norwich
NR1 1RY
Tel: 01603 611811
e-mail: taxassist.co.uk
Web site: www.taxassist.co.uk
Contact: Mrs L Charleton

Business description: Accountancy and financial assistance to small
businesses
BFA membership: Provisional
No. of franchise outlets: 54
Year business started: 1995

Start-up capital (minimum): £15,000
Initial fee: £11,750
Management fee: 9%
Proportion of start-up capital that can be arranged: 50% (through high
street banks)

Additional information: We are the market leader providing
accountancy and self-assessment assistance in a professional manner to
small businesses. Marketing and technical training followed by
continuous support.

Techclean Services
VDU House
Old Kiln Lane
Churt
Farnham
Surrey
GU10 2JH
Tel: 01428 713713
Freephone: 0800 281940
Fax: 01428 713798
e-mail: techclean@easynet.co.uk
Web site: www.techclean.com.uk
Contact: D Cooper

Business description: Cleaning of hi-tech equipment
BFA membership: No
No. of franchise outlets: 52 UK, 20 overseas
Year business started: 1987

Start-up capital (minimum): £10,000
Initial fee: £13,500
Management fee: 15% of turnover
Proportion of start-up capital that can be arranged: 50%

Temples Estate Management (UK) Ltd
12 Bank Street
Norwich
NR2 4SE
Tel: 01603 661170
e-mail: templeship@aol.com
Web site: www.visualise.com/temples
Contact: David L Temple
Business description: Residential property letting and management
BFA membership: Provisional
No. of franchise outlets: 7
Year business started: 1965

Start-up capital (minimum): £15,000–£20,000
Initial fee: £12,500 plus VAT
Management fee: 8.5%
Proportion of start-up capital that can be arranged: Nil

Thrifty Car Rental
The Old Court House
Hughenden Road
High Wycombe
Buckinghamshire
HP13 5DT
Tel: 01494 751500
e-mail: flightfm@thrifty.co.uk
Web site: n/a
Contact: Graham Bullock

Business description: Franchisor car and van rental
BFA membership: Full
No. of franchise outlets: 68
Year business started: 1990

Start-up capital (minimum): £80,000
Initial fee: £17,500 plus VAT
Management fee: 5%
Proportion of start-up capital that can be arranged: 70% maximum

Tongue Tied Ltd
Savan House
49 Goldstone Villas
Hove
BN3 3RT
Tel: 01273 723988
e-mail: sales@tongue-tied.co.uk
Web site: http://www.tongue-tied.co.uk
Contact: John Shouler

Business description: Translation and interpreting services
BFA membership: No
No. of franchise outlets: 5
Year business started: 1989 (Tongue Tied UK franchised 1997)

Start-up capital (minimum): £5,000
Initial fee: £6,995
Management fee: Nil
Proportion of start-up capital that can be arranged: 100%

Travail Employment Group Ltd
24 Southgate Street
Gloucester
GL1 2DP
Tel: 01452 420700
e-mail: n/a
Web site: http://www.travail.co.uk
Contact: Mr Steve Mills

Business description: Temporary and permanent recruitment services
BFA membership: Full
No. of franchise outlets: 40
Year business started: 1977

Start-up capital (minimum): £65,000
Initial fee: £10,000
Management fee: 7.25% of sales
Proportion of start-up capital that can be arranged: £45,000

Tumble Tots (UK) Ltd
Blue Bird Park
Bromsgrove Road
Hunnington
Halesowen
West Midlands
B62 0TT
Tel: 0121 585 7003
Fax: 0121 585 6891
e-mail: tumbletots.uk@btinternet.com
Web site: n/a
Contact: David Hunt

Business description: Active physical play for pre-school children
BFA membership: No
No. of franchise outlets: 80
Year business started: 1979

Start-up capital (minimum): £15,500 (plus working capital and vehicle)
Initial fee: £5,800 (licence fee for 2 years)
Management fee: Licence is then renewed annually and an annual fee
is payable.
Proportion of start-up capital that can be arranged: Major banks may
provide up to 67%

Urban Planters

202 Pasture Lane
Bradford
BD7 2SE
Tel: 01274 579331
e-mail: anything@urbanplanters.co.uk
Web site: n/a
Contact: Nick Gresty

Business description: Rental and maintenance of indoor plants
BFA membership: Provisional
No. of franchise outlets: 8
Year business started: 1965

Start-up capital (minimum): £50,000 (includes £20,000 working capital)
Initial fee: £12,000
Management fee: 7.5% of sales invoiced
Proportion of start-up capital that can be arranged: 70% maximum

User2 Franchising Ltd

Unit 10
Greencroft Industrial Park
Annfield Plain
Co. Durham DH9 7YB
Tel: 01207 524700
e-mail: franchise@user2.co.uk
Web site: n/a
Contact: Allan Mitchell

Business description: Computer retail store
BFA membership: Provisional
No. of franchise outlets: 2
Year business started: 1995

Start-up capital (minimum): £110,000
Initial fee: £12,500
Management fee: 6%
Proportion of start-up capital that can be arranged: 70%

Val-U-Pak
Clare Lodge
41 Holly Bush Lane
Harpenden
AL5 4AY
Tel: 01582 462744
e-mail: franchise@val-u-pak.com
Web site: n/a
Contact: Jeff Frankling

Business description: Local community discount vouchers
BFA membership: No
No. of franchise outlets: 3
Year business started: 1987

Start-up capital (minimum): £1,500
Initial fee: £1,500
Management fee: 10% (£40 monthly minimum)
Proportion of start-up capital that can be arranged: Nil

Ventrolla Ltd
11 Hornbeam Square South
South Harrogate
North Yorkshire
HG2 8NB
Tel: 01423 870011
Fax: 01423 873399
e-mail: info@ventrolla.co.uk
Web site: www.ventrolla.co.uk
Contact: Mrs Lesley Spence (Marketing Manager)

Business description: Sash window renovation specialists
BFA membership: Associate
No. of franchise outlets: 17
Year business started: 1985

Start-up capital (minimum): £15,000
Initial fee: £15,500
Management fee: 10% of sales
Proportion of start-up capital that can be arranged: 50% (£20,000)

VIP Bin Cleaning Ltd
5 Frensham Road
Sweet Briar Business Park
Norwich
NR3 2BT
Tel: 01603 412030
e-mail: vipbin@globalnet.co.uk
Web site: www.lds.co.uk/franchise/vip
Contact: Mark Harvey

Business description: Wheelie-bin cleaning
BFA membership: Associate
No. of franchise outlets: 40
Year business started: 1995

Start-up capital (minimum): £10,500
Initial fee: £7,500
Management fee: £75 per week
Proportion of start-up capital that can be arranged: 70% approx.

Wicked Wheels International Ltd
PO Box 5066
Leighton Buzzard
LU7 7YS
Tel: 0800 298 5454
e-mail: wicked.wheels@dial.pipex.com
Web site: n/a
Contact: Stephen Wood

Business description: Mobile alloy wheel restoration
BFA membership: No
No. of franchise outlets: 3
Year business started: 1998

Start-up capital (minimum): £30,000
Initial fee: £25,000
Management fee: 10% royalties
Proportion of start-up capital that can be arranged: 70%

Worldwide Refinishing Systems
Spectrum House
Lower Oakham Way
Oakham Business Park
Mansfield
NG18 5BY
Tel: 01623 422439
e-mail: n/a
Web site: n/a
Contact: Phil Else

Business description: Bath refinishing/bathroom remodelling
BFA membership: No
No. of franchise outlets: 20
Year business started: UK 1990

Start-up capital (minimum): £10,000
Initial fee: £18,000
Management fee: 8% of gross turnover
Proportion of start-up capital that can be arranged: 80%

Additional information: Franchise is part of Dwyer Group, Texas.

Zenith Concepts Ltd (Blimpie, Ireland)
14a Avenue Road
Lurgan
Co. Armagh
Northern Ireland
BT66 7BB
Tel: 01762 322202/348777
e-mail: clive@zenco.com
roger@zenco.com
Web site: n/a
Contact: Clive Turkington, Roger Turkington

Business description: American sandwich franchise
BFA membership: No
No. of franchise outlets: About to commence build-out on no. 1
Year business started: 1997 – Blimpie licence purchased

Start-up capital (minimum): From £35,000
Initial fee: £6,000–£12,000
Management fee: 8% royalties plus 2% for advertising (of turnover)
Proportion of start-up capital that can be arranged: Nil

12 UK Growth and Opportunities

MARKET FACTORS

The factors that fuelled the growth of franchising in the 1990s were divided between changes in the economic and in the political climates. The recession of the early 1990s generated more people with large redundancy payments, who elected after losing their job to go into business for themselves instead. Franchising seemed to offer a way of combining the independence of self-employment with the security of a proven business formula.

Table 12.1 *How franchising has grown*

Year	Annual sales, £bn	Number of units	Jobs created
1986	1.9	10,900	126,000
1987	3.1	15,000	169,000
1988	3.8	16,000	181,500
1989	4.7	16,600	185,000
1990	5.2	18,260	184,000
1991	4.8	18,600	189,500
1992	4.5	18,100	184,000
1993	5.0	24,900	188,500
1994	5.5	26,400	192,300
1995	5.9	25,700	212,200
1996	6.2	27,100	228,000
1997	7.0	29,100	235,000

Source: NatWest/BFA survey

Market factors have helped too. The growth in popularity of fast food as a result of changing lifestyles, for example, has helped to stimulate demand for franchised food outlets. The growing number of women entering work has encouraged demand for dry cleaning services, home help agencies and the emergence of US-style convenience stores which meet a need for early and late shopping in neighbourhood areas.

The government has also increasingly recognised the importance of new businesses in job creation and economic growth. This has led to a range of stimulatory measures aimed at the small business sector in general, but with an inevitable overspill that has benefited the franchise sector.

The banks, accountancy firms and legal practices have also worked in their various ways to legitimise franchising and to encourage and advise would-be franchisees.

Business format franchising in the UK is forecast to top £8 billion by the year 2000, with most sectors experiencing some growth. Ahead in the growth league will be service-type operations and those franchises with a relatively low entry cost.

SUCCESS STORIES

As well as the Body Shop, a number of other franchises were conspicuously successful in the late eighties.

Tie Rack has expanded from a tiny shop in London's Oxford Street to become one of Britain's most exciting retail outlets, with over 100 franchises throughout the country. On the back of this success, Roy Bishko, Tie Rack's founder and chairman, was able to raise £1.5 million expansion capital in June 1986 from Midland Bank and its merchant banking subsidiary, Samuel Montagu. The same year saw the successful launch of the Sock Shop, with applications for shares far exceeding supply. The Sock Shop chose not to franchise its chain and many cite that as a reason for the problems it experienced under its first ownership.

Interlink, another franchise quoted on the Stock Exchange, was valued at £30 million when it was floated. In the three years to 1986, Interlink's turnover grew from £4.5 to £13.7 million, while pre-tax profits soared some 600 per cent from £372,000 to £2.59 million.

In 1988, Thorntons brought its 201 company-owned shops and 92 franchised outlets to the stock market at a value of £78.6 million. At the same time Levi Strauss, the jeans manufacturer, announced the launch of 50 franchise shops in Britain.

The depressed economic climate of the early nineties has seen stock market activity generally decline, with very few new businesses coming to the market.

One company that was already on the market before it began franchising is Cullen Holdings, the up-market convenience store. After years of losses and failed strategies, the group took to franchising in 1990 and by June 1991 store turnover had climbed 40 per cent and loss-making outlets had become profitable. The group has paid its first dividend since 1984. The key to Cullens' success is the motivation of its franchisees. With no price advantage and services competition from Asian-owned corner stores, franchising is the strategic difference that has saved Cullens from failure.

Pizza Express came to the stock market in February 1993, after 28 years in business. The chain consists of 13 company-owned outlets and 52 franchised outlets. Peter Boizot, the founder and chairman, netted about £10 million from the deal.

In 1994 Finelist, the automotive products group, came to the stock market. The company has 73 outlets including 25 franchises, and its 1993 turnover was £16 million, with profits of £1.2 million. The float raised £6 million of new money, which is being used to finance a further 50 outlets.

In late 1998, quoted franchisors were suffering as much, if not more than, other retailers. The Body Shop experienced a major set-back in France, where its franchise network failed to take off in the manner expected, and Tie Rack saw its profits halve.

PROBLEMS

It has not been all plain sailing in the franchise world over the last few years.

On 15 October 1985 the eighth UK Convention of Young's Franchise Group Ltd was held at the Grand Hotel, Brighton, and attended by a representative of Barclays Bank, the group's major creditor. No indication was given at the Convention that the group might be in a parlous condition.

One month later, on Friday, 10 November 1985, the Young's Franchise Group, consisting of Young's Formal Hire, Pronuptia Wedding Hire and the new La Mama fashion maternity wear chain, went into receivership without warning, with debts of £3.75 million.

Ten days later, on 25 November, Young's was sold to Cyril Spencer, former chairman of the Burton Group, for £1.5 million. After preferential creditors such as the Inland Revenue and National Insurance took their slice, what was left went to Barclays Bank, which even then was substantially out of pocket on the deal.

Many of the Young Group's franchisees suffered as a result of this débâcle, none more than the holders of La Mama franchises. All but six of the former 23 franchises have closed, many forced out of business by crippling debts, in a venture which the new management have subsequently said was inadequately researched.

The Young Group was a senior member of the British Franchise Association.

The 333 franchisees of Homelocaters UK, a national flat finding agency, were even less fortunate. In May 1986 Homelocators UK was convicted, as a limited company, of breaching the 1953 Accommodation Agencies Act, and ordered to pay £1550 in fines and compensation. Attempts to find the franchise founders to serve a distress warrant for the cash met with no success. Homelocators were not a member of the British Franchise Association.

The Cookie Coach Company, whose franchisees sold cakes and cookies from 1920s' style vans, was compulsorily wound up at the request of the Department of Trade and Industry. On 3 December 1986, Peat Marwick, the accountancy firm, was appointed receiver of the company with the task of selling the business as a going concern. The likely deficiency when the dust settled was over half a million pounds. Cookie Coach Company was not a member of the BFA, but it was on the BFA Register of Qualified Non-Member Companies, developing a franchise. The company is now run by Carr Foods.

Since 1988 there has been a rise in the percentage of franchised units operating which either were commercial failures, or which withdrew from franchising. The figures are still quite small when compared with failure in the small business sector as a whole, where figures of 15 to 30 per cent are frequently quoted.

Among recent failures is TAXSCOL which was set up in 1986 to offer a computerised tax form filling service. In the summer of 1990 the business disintegrated leaving its 25 franchisees, many accountants and tax experts themselves, to battle to recover their investment.

The prospects of £40,000 in the first year drew hundreds of enquiries, but TAXSCOL founders, Dorothy Grant and her husband Robert, were unable to deliver and their former franchisees took their cases through the high courts in 1991. Four have won awards totalling £50,000, but no money is yet forthcoming.

In July 1991 Alan Paul, the trendy Liverpudlian hairdressing group, unveiled an impressive increase in pre-tax profits for the year – up 200 per cent to £3.74 million. A string of acquisitions gave a tremendous boost to both profits and turnover. They were all set to move up from the USM to a full stock market quote. The company had 437 salons, 87 cosmetic shops trading under the name The Body and Face Place, and 13 Blue Berry's Brasseries.

On 5 December the same year, bankers to Alan Paul appointed Ernst & Young as receivers. Within days Essanelle, bought for £8.3 million 12 months earlier, had been sold to a German investment company for an undisclosed sum. Overall the company appeared to have negative value and the way in which Alan Paul ran its franchises is the subject of an independent financial inquiry by Coopers & Lybrand Deloitte. Many franchisees are now facing severe financial difficulties.

In 1992 there were 33 failures among franchisors. Quill Wills, a company selling will-writing franchises, holds something of a record for failure. When it closed in 1993, it was the third Quill company to stop trading in two years. The group is alleged to have misrepresented potential earnings. Some 45 franchises were in operation.

Even conspicuous success in other fields does not guarantee that an entrepreneur can hack it as a franchisor. Howard Hodgson, the 42-year-old businessman who made a fortune out of funeral parlours, and then wrote his autobiography, *How to Become Dead Rich*, had to fold up his accounting franchise. Prontac, his franchise chain set up in 1992, sold nearly 80 franchises for between £12,000 and £17,000.

Athena, the franchise chain subsidiary of the publicly quoted Pentos group, collapsed at the end of 1994. The 127 company-owned shops were closed down by the receiver. Half of the franchised shops, 16 in all, were bought out by the former franchisees, but the business is certainly not the same one that they went into at the outset.

In 1997 Burger King had to withdraw from France, closing 50 franchises in the face of overwhelming competition from McDonald's.

Franchise casualties

At the system level, a total of 47 withdrawals have been identified, compared to 69 in the last NatWest/BFA report. Just three of these are attributable to commercial failure, while the others have either been taken over or have chosen not to pursue the franchising option further for various reasons. For the general health of franchising, such changes do mean that opportunities continue to appear for new systems that may be better equipped to prosper in these market areas.

It is by no means the case that, when a system fails, all of the franchisees go down with it. In many cases the individual units continue to trade successfully. Even if they may now be outside a franchise system, many such businesses owe their continued success to what the franchise system originally offered them.

At the individual unit level, not surprisingly, the position is somewhat more volatile.

Unit changes reported by franchisors

	Changed franchisee	Bought back	Closed down	Sold/left franchising	Total
All	880	290	1,060	170	2,400
Reasons:					
– Commercial failure	130	70	410	20	630
– Dispute	30	20	60	10	120
– Other reasons	720	200	590	140	1650

These figures indicate that about 2.6 per cent of units have undergone some form of change for reasons of commercial failure and 0.5 per cent owing to a dispute between the franchisor and the franchisee, giving a total of 3.1 per cent for these two reasons. When added together with the buy-backs, closures and sell-offs completed for other reasons, plus an estimate for the units going down in system failures, it is reckoned that 7 per cent of all franchised units operating a year ago have undergone some 'forced' change. This is an encouraging improvement on the figure for last year which was 7.4 per cent.

$\boxed{13}$ International Opportunities

GLOBAL MARKET-PLACE

Most big businesses today see themselves as operating in a global market-place. Some firms, such as those operating in Australia, have little option but to look beyond their relatively small number of indigenous customers if they are to achieve substantial growth. Franchising is no exception to this trend.

While the USA is the biggest franchise market in the world, it is not the only one – nor perhaps the one with the greatest potential.

Global distribution of franchisors and franchisees

Country	Franchisors	Franchisees
United States	3,000	250,00
Canada	1,000	65,000
Brazil	932	60,000
Japan	714	139,788
Australia/NZ	600	26,000
France	520	30,000
Germany	500	18,000
Britain	414	26,400
Italy	400	18,500
Mexico	375	18,724
Netherlands	341	11,975
Spain	280	18,500

Austria	200	3,000
Hungary	200	10,000
Sweden	200	9,000
Norway	185	3,500
Belgium	150	3,083
Malaysia	125	800
Argentina	100	3,500
Singapore	85	1,600
Finland	70	900
Denmark	68	1,210
Philippines	56	61
Colombia	48	300
Chile	45	25
Yugoslavia	45	620
Czech Republic	35	100
Israel	18	15
Bulgaria	0	7
Total	10,706	720,608

Source: Swartz, L N (1995) _Worldwide Franchising Statistics: A study of worldwide franchise associations_, Arthur Andersen in co-operation with the World Franchising Council, Chicago, Ill.

WHY FRANCHISORS ARE GOING INTERNATIONAL

From the small town of Temecula in Southern California to the streets of Cairo is not so great a leap as one might imagine. Chico's Tacos made it when they opened their first overseas store, in the Egyptian capital, though it is too soon to tell how this Mexican fare will sell in the Nile Valley.

To go or not to go overseas is a question more franchisors are pondering as potentially lucrative, sometimes wide-open foreign markets beckon. About 400 of the US's 3,500 franchisors – about 11 per cent – are doing business abroad, according to the International Franchise Association in Washington, DC. Significantly, an additional 1,000 have said in IFA surveys that they plan to award franchises abroad within five years.

Probably the best evidence of this international growth is that overseas markets – for years the province of the US's largest franchisors – are being targeted by smaller, newer companies like the 100-unit Chico's, which began franchising domestically only three years ago.

Generally the factors leading the US businesses to look for opportunities abroad are also driving franchising's international expansion. Those factors include heightened awareness of global markets, relaxation of trade barriers, saturation of some existing domestic markets, increasing prosperity and demand for consumer goods in many regions overseas, and increasing ease of doing business internationally because of improved communications and transportation systems.

In addition, franchisors are benefiting from the growing awareness of franchising as a concept in countries where it was virtually unknown only a few years ago.

Brands are going global

For franchisors, one of the biggest benefits is name recognition. A brand name brings confidence, credibility and value to the consumer. For example, if a consumer had the choice between staying at a no-name hotel or a Days Inn hotel or a Holiday Inn which would he or she choose? Which one is more likely to have consistent quality? Which one is more likely to offer predictable value?

In the United States, the brands have created top-of-mind awareness among consumers, and that has had spillover abroad. People outside the United States have heard of major brands, and franchisors are now working to create consumer preferences towards those brands by establishing a presence abroad.

TECHNOLOGY

Communication is the lifeblood of franchise systems. If information doesn't flow efficiently between headquarters and franchisees, friction and chaos are virtually inevitable.

American Leak Detection, based in Palm Springs, California,

intuitively understands the way that bad information pipelines can turn a good franchise business into a bad dream. The rapidly growing operation has 135 owners in seven countries, including Brazil, Spain, Saudi Arabia, Australia, Canada and the UK. But even with high-tech fibre optic telephone links, conventional voice lines simply weren't doing the job.

Like an increasing number of franchisors, American Leak Detection found a tool to help it build a global system for moving information effectively: the Internet's World Wide Web. The Internet and the technologies it has spawned are proving potent ways for companies selling everything from plumbing services to sandwiches to build more efficient, effective and intimate links with both franchisees and consumers. A franchisee in Brazil can communicate effectively and daily with their franchisor in the United States.

In the same way as it has reached into so many other areas of business life, the Internet is transforming the way franchisors and franchisees work with each other. It is allowing them to create simple, easy-to-use systems that enable stores and headquarters to tear down communication barriers between countries and continents at a relatively low cost.

HOW CAN FRANCHISEES BENEFIT?

There are three clear opportunities for the alert franchisee or prospective franchisee to exploit in the arena of international business opportunities:

- ☐ One approach, called direct franchising, is to seek out individuals abroad who are interested in operating franchised businesses in their own countries.
- ☐ Another method is to pursue a joint venture with another company, which usually results in the formation of a third company owned by both partners to handle operations in a particular region.
- ☐ A more typical approach, though, is the one used by the vast majority of US franchisors – namely, finding and training

master franchisees, typically well-capitalised business people who understand the local laws and market-place.

A master franchisee buys the rights to develop units within an area or a country. Usually, the territory is an entire country. After establishing a successful track record, the franchisee may be granted additional territories. For example, a master franchisee with TCBY International, the yogurt company based in Little Rock, Arkansas, opened 21 stores in China and Hong Kong and was then given the go-ahead to develop the brand in India. The franchisee has contracted with an Indian dairy products company to set up at least 25 stores within five years.

Each approach to expanding internationally has advantages and drawbacks. Direct franchising requires more franchisor involvement but gives the franchisor much greater control over the foreign operation.

Joint ventures create more cumbersome tax and financial issues than the other two approaches. Master franchising is popular because it requires minimal franchisor cost and less direct franchisor involvement. A master franchisee provides local expertise and oversight of the sub-franchisees whom it chooses to operate individual stores.

Master franchises are advertised in newspapers and franchise publications, or by trade missions, and international brokers. Another good source of candidates is the US Department of Commerce, which seeks out foreign partners for US companies through its Gold Key programme.

An example of master franchise advertisements is shown below.

ATTENTION ENTREPRENEURS!

We are specialists in developing franchise opportunities worldwide and have been retained by a number of our major North American franchisor clients to assist them to locate master franchisees and area developers who can develop their concepts in the UK and/or Europe. They seek entrepreneurs and organisations who have capital available in the region of £100,000 to £2 million.

Bojangles
(come taste the difference)

'Bojangles the Cajun Chicken Company'

One of North America's most highly developed fast food restaurant franchise networks, Bojangles provides a powerful brand identity. This offers the potential to become a brand as dynamic in the UK as any of the established North American fast food franchises. When coupled with the expertise, experience, training and support that will be provided, this has to be one of the most outstanding opportunities in the fast food sector currently available for the UK – now seeking area developers.

Teriyaki Experience

'Made in Japan Teriyaki Experience'

The largest Japanese fast food restaurant chain in Canada. Providing meals similar to that of expensive Japanese sit-down restaurants but with fast food pricing and service. This unique fast food operation will allow an investor to capitalise on the increasing awareness of Japanese cuisine. The focus on fresh vegetables, yakisoba noodles, meats, seafood and sushi will ensure demand from UK consumers seeking a healthy and innovative eating experience. The UK master franchisee will receive the benefits of established and proven operating systems, comprehensive initial training and ongoing support, branded, high-quality, easy-to-prepare food products and dynamic marketing resources.

Candleman

This stylish and sophisticated candle and accessory retail concept is the dominant player of its type in the North American market. There is considerable potential to replicate that status in the UK and European markets. A highly developed identity coupled with the training and support of a management team with 200 combined years of retail and franchise experience will provide an excellent opportunity for the investor who recognises the potential of this concept. The unique visual identity of this high profit margin retail operation can only really be appreciated by a study of the master franchise prospectus.

Be aggressive

You don't have to wait for franchisors to advertise. You can go and seek them out. For example, Party Land, Inc., a party supply chain based in Plymouth Meeting, PA, receives 20 to 30 inquiries a month from potential franchisees. The company looks for more than money, it sees whether master franchisees have a service-conscious approach – the ability to understand what they are doing.

Party Land's first location abroad, in Singapore, was initiated when holiday-makers from Singapore saw a Party Land store in Pennsylvania and asked the company about developing the concept.

Another franchisor that was prompted by a potential master franchisee to enter the global market-place is American Fastsigns, based in Carrollton, Texas. The company, which has more than $70 million in revenues, now has its custom sign and lettering stores in seven countries. In Brazil alone it has opened 11 stores and plans for a total of 60 there within the next five years. The company's foreign expansion has been achieved mainly through master franchisees, although it has awarded individual franchises directly in Canada and Mexico.

Playing away

It is possible for a potential franchisor – or master franchisor – to set up shop outside their home market. The Body Shop's first master franchisor in France, for example, was not French.

Some highly flexible arrangements, such as that adopted by Cabouchon, allow their 'agents' to sell in any country to anybody, rather as many insurance companies allow their sales agents to operate with known contacts rather than defined geography. But this is a fairly exceptional phenomenon, open only to the most adventurous, or those who truly know their market.

EVALUATING INTERNATIONAL MARKETS

If you do feel the urge to exploit international opportunities, which market should you go for? This table was produced by the US Department of Commerce to give franchisors pointers as to where to look for master franchisors. By their criteria the UK is quite an attractive area for American franchisors to set up in.

Foreign Franchise Markets

Figures are US millions; 5 on the scale means 'very' or 'significant', 1 means 'negligible' or 'none'.

Country	Total value of franchise goods and sevices sold	Total goods and services from US franchises	Market receptivity to franchising	Competition from other franchises in the same sector	Market barriers (Gov'mt Rules)
Canada	76,436	40,749	5	2	2
Japan	65,100	1,890	4	3	3
France	29,000	580	4	1	4
Germany	10,500	900	4	4	2
United Kingdom	8,750	–	4	3	5
Italy	6,500	350	4	3	4
Mexico	5,350	3,500	5	5	5
Norway	4,800	70	5	3	5
Brazil	4,200	640	5	4	3
Belgium	3,000	310	4	2	4
Switzerland	2,200	870	4	4	3
Singapore	630	440	5	4	5
Hong Kong	600	350	5	4	5
Spain	500	350	5	4	5
Sweden	500	152	3	3	5
Finland	390	50	3	2	4
Saudi Arabia	185	125	4	3	4
Nigeria	25	0	5	5	3
India	15	0	3	2	3
Taiwan	13	4	4	2	4
Thailand	6	5	5	5	5

Source: International Trade Administration, US Department of Commerce

These global figures hide a host of segment- and industry-based opportunities for would-be master franchisees and direct franchisees alike.

For example, the Japanese 'mom and pop' dominated restaurant business has one eaterie per 125 Japanese consumers vs. one per 400 Americans. Also, paternalistic Japanese employers have heavily subsidised food service as a worker benefit in the recession as an added incentive to retain staff. So Japan's fast food franchising industry has blossomed, faster than other sectors of the economy.

LEGAL ISSUES

The growth of franchising around the world has led to an inevitable proliferation of laws governing it. Until 1988, franchising was regulated on a national level only in the United States. Since then, various franchising laws have taken effect in 20 countries.

In 1988, the 12 countries in the European Community, now the European Union, adopted the Block Exemption on Franchising, which exempts franchise companies from the EU's anti-trust laws. Since then, France, Mexico and Brazil have enacted laws similar to those of the United States, requiring franchisors to provide pre-sale disclosure to prospective franchisees.

Australia and Italy have adopted voluntary codes pertaining to pre-sale disclosure and other requirements. In addition to laws specifically governing franchising, a wide range of other statutes may affect franchising in various countries. They cover trademarks, anti-trust issues, taxes, contracts, technology transfer, currency control, foreign investment, and import and export restrictions.

The most important legal issues covering franchising are:

1. *Trademarks*. Because piracy is a problem in some countries, trademark registration should be the first item of international business. It is not uncommon for a company wishing to expand abroad to discover that someone else has already applied to register its trademark.

Ideally, a company should start the registration process one to two years before entering a market. That includes meeting a trademark lawyer, considering which countries to enter, and beginning the actual filing process. The business reality, though, is that when an opportunity to enter a market presents itself, trademark registration must be handled quickly.

For the potential direct or master franchisee, it is important to make sure the franchisor has this area covered.

2. *Local laws.* Some foreign jurisdictions require the franchisor to pay termination fees to a franchisee when the franchise arrangement is being ended. Others restrict certain foreigners from operating certain types of businesses (a prohibition that could apply to a prospective franchisee), or they may restrict the outflow of hard foreign currency. In Greece for example there are rules against selling magazines within a certain distance of the ubiquitous magazine kiosks. In Greece a franchisee also has a legal right to terminate the franchise if the franchisor has engaged in 'insulting behaviour'.

3. *Dispute-resolution provisions.* Because foreign courts have no obligation to enforce a judgment from a court against a foreign party, contracts should contain a clause outlining the means of dispute resolution, which is usually arbitration.

Many countries abide by a multilateral UN treaty on recognition and enforcement of arbitration awards rendered in the signatory countries. Contracts should designate the location and ruling authority of any arbitration proceedings.

If you are going to get involved with an international partner you must understand the legal rules governing your contract.

14 The British Franchise Association

The British Franchise Association made major changes to it membership criteria in 1990 and the main elements of membership now centre on demonstration of the substance of the franchised business. Applicants for full membership must now prove that their business is viable, franchisable, ethical and disclosed and that their franchise network has a proven trading and franchising record. Regular checks, and accreditation every two years, will ensure the maintenance of standards. Also under the new rules, members must allow access to confidential information by a duly authorised member of BFA staff.

The changes have the effect of tightening controls over BFA members and ensuring that the franchise network has longevity and continuity.

It should be borne in mind that, although franchising substantially reduces the inherent risk in a new business venture, it does not automatically guarantee success. At the same time, registration with or membership of this or any other association does not automatically protect the member company, or his franchisee, against commercial failure.

The BFA administrative office is at Thames View, Newtown Road, Henley-on-Thames, Oxfordshire RG9 1HG (tel: 01491 578049; fax 01491 573517; e-mail: mailroom@british-franchise.org.uk; www.british-franchise.org.uk).

FULL MEMBERS

Franchisors are required to submit a completed application form, including disclosure document, franchise agreement, prospectus, accounts, etc, and provide proof of a correctly constituted pilot scheme successfully operated for at least one year, financed and managed by the applicant company. In addition, evidence of successful franchising over a subsequent two-year period with at least four franchisees is required.

Alldays
Alldays House
Cheshunt Avenue
Chandlers Ford
Southampton SO53 3HJ

Alphagraphics
Thornburgh Road
Eastfield
Scarborough YO11 3UY

Amtrak Express Parcels Ltd
Company House
Tower Hill
Bristol BS2 0AZ

Apollo Window Blinds Ltd
Cold Heseldon Industrial
Estate
Seaham
County Durham SR7 8ST

Autela Components Ltd
Regal House
Birmingham Road
Stratford-upon-Avon
Warwickshire CV37 0BN

**Budget Rent-a-Car
International Inc.**
41 Marlowes
Hemel Hempstead
Hertfordshire HP1 1LD

Card Connection Ltd
Park House
South Street
Farnham
Surrey GU9 7QQ

**Chem-Dry Northern &
Southern Ltd**
Colonial House
Swinemoor Lane
Beverley
East Riding of Yorkshire
HU17 0LS

Chem-Dry UK (Midlands &
London)
Unit 4 Mercian Park
Felspar Road
Amington Industrial Estate
Tamworth
Staffordshire B77 4DP

Chemical Express Ltd
Spring Road
Smethwick
West Midlands B66 1PT

City Link (*see* **Initial City Link Ltd**)

Clarks Shoes
40 High Street
Street
Somerset BA16 0YA

Colour Counsellors Ltd
3 Dovedale Studios
465 Battersea Park Road
London SW11 4LR

Computa Tune
Oxford Street
Accrington
Lancashire BB5 1QX

Dairy Crest
Woburn House
Duke Street
Luton
Bedfordshire LU2 0HJ

Dampcure Woodcure
Darley House
41 Merton Road
Watford
Hertfordshire WD1 7BU

Dominos Pizza
Unit 10 Maryland Road
Tongwell
Milton Keynes MK15 8HF

Drain Doctor Ltd
Franchise House
Adam Court
Newark Road
Peterborough
Cambridgeshire PE1 5PP

Driver Hire
Progress House
Castlefields Lane
Bingley
West Yorkshire BD16 2AB

Durham Pine
Colima Avenue
Hilton Riverside
Sunderland SR5 3XF

Dyno-Rod Developments Ltd
143 Maple Road
Surbiton
Surrey KT6 4BJ

Dyno-Rod plc
Zockoll House
143 Maple Road
Surbiton
Surrey KY6 4BJ

Express Dairies plc
Raines House
Denby Dale Road
Wakefield WF1 1HR

Francesco Group
Woodings Yard
Bailey Street
Staffordshire ST17 4BG

Greenalls Inn Partnership
Greenalls Avenue
PO Box No 2
Warrington
Cheshire WA4 6RH

**Humana International Group
plc**
Humana House
11 Eton High Street
Eton
Berkshire SL4 6AT

Initial City Link Ltd
Batavia Road
Sunbury-on-Thames
Middlesex TW16 5LR

Interlink Express Parcels Ltd
Brunswick Court
Brunswick Square
Bristol BS2 8PE

In-Toto Ltd
Wakefield Road
Gildersome
Leeds LS27 7JZ

Kall-Kwik Printing (UK) Ltd
Kall-Kwik House
106 Pembroke Road
Ruislip
Middlesex HA4 8NW

**Legal & General Estate
Agency**
7 Low Ousegate
York
YO1 9QX

Master Thatchers Ltd
Faircross Offices
Stratfield Saye
Reading
Berkshire RG7 2BT

McDonald's Restaurants Ltd
11–59 High Road
East Finchley
London N2 8AW

Mercury Express
2nd Floor Suite
54 Hamilton Square
Birkenhead
Wirral L41 5AS

Metro-Rod plc
Metro House
Churchill Way
Macclesfield
Cheshire SK11 6AY

Minster Services Group UK
Minster House
948–952 Kingsbury Road
Erdington
Birmingham B24 9PZ

Molly Maid UK
Vale House
100 Vale Road
Windsor
Berkshire SL4 5JL

Mr Clutch
2 Priory Road
Strood
Rochester
Kent ME2 2EG

**Nationwide Investigations
Group Ltd**
86 Southwark Bridge Road
London SE1 0EX

**Neal's Yard (Natural
Remedies) Ltd**
26–34 Ingate Place
Battersea
London SW8 3NS

PDC Copyprint
1 Church Lane
East Grinstead
West Sussex RH19 3AZ

Perfect Pizza
Units 5 & 6 The Forum
Hanworth Lane
Chertsey
Surrey KT16 9JX

Pirtek (Europe) plc
35 Acton Park Estate
The Vale
Acton
London W3 7QE

Pitman Training Group plc
Pitman House
Audby Lane
Wetherby
West Yorkshire LS22 7FD

Post Office Counters Ltd
2nd Floor
King Edward Building
King Edward Street
London EC1A 1AA

Practical Car & Van Rental
21–23 Little Broom Street
Camp Hill
Birmingham B12 0EU

Prontaprint Ltd
Axis 6
Rhodes Way
North Watford Industrial
Estate
Watford WD2 4YW

**Rainbow International Carpet
Dyeing & Cleaning Company**
Spectrum House
Lower Oakham Way
Oakham Business Park
Mansfield
Nottinghamshire NG18 5BY

Recognition Express Ltd
PO Box 7
Rugby Road
Hinckley
Leicestershire LE10 2NE

Ribbon Revival Ltd
Casion Court
Pitronnerie Road
St Peter Port
Guernsey GY1 2RW

Safeclean International
152 Milton Park
Abingdon
Oxfordshire OX14 4SD

Saks Hair (Holdings)
Ltd/Command Performance
2 Peel Court
St Cuthbert's Way
Darlington
Co. Durham DL1 1GB

Securicor Omega Express-
Sameday
Comewell House
North Street
Horsham
West Sussex BN12 1BQ

ServiceMaster Ltd
ServiceMaster House
Leicester Road
Anstey
Leicestershire LE7 7AT

Signs Express Ltd
The Old Church
St Matthew's Road
Norwich NR1 1SP

Snap-on-Tools Ltd
Telford Way
Kettering
Northamptonshire NN16 8SN

Snappy Snaps Franchises Ltd
12 Glenthorne Mews
115 Glenthorne Road
London W6 0LJ

Spud-U-Like Ltd
9 Central Business Centre
Great Central Way
London NW10 0UR

Student Support Centre (UK)
Ltd
46 Church Avenue
Beckenham
Kent BR3 1DT

The Flat Roof Company
Unit 7C, Guardian Park
Station Industrial Estate
Tadcaster
N. Yorkshire LS24 9SG

Thorntons
J W Thornton Ltd
Thornton Park
Somercotes
Derby DE55 4XJ

Thrifty Car Rental
The Old Courthouse
Hughendon Road
High Wycombe
Buckinghamshire HP13 5DT

Toni & Guy
Tigi House
Central Way
North Feltham Trading Estate
Feltham
Middlesex TW14 0QZ

Travail Employment Group Ltd
24 Southgate Street
Gloucester
GL1 2DP

Unigate Dairies Ltd
14–40 Victoria Road
Aldershot
Hampshire GU11 1TH

Vendo plc
215 East Lane
Wembley
Middlesex HA0 3NG

Wimpy International Ltd
2 The Listons
Liston Road
Marlow
Buckinghamshire SL7 1FD

REGISTER OF ASSOCIATES

Franchisors are required to submit a completed application form, including disclosure document, franchise agreement, prospectus, accounts etc, and provide proof of a correctly constituted pilot scheme successfully operated for at least one year, financed and managed by the applicant company (as for full membership) but with evidence of successful franchising for a period of one year with at least one franchisee.

Auditel
39 Southgate Street
Winchester
Hampshire SO23 9EH

Blazes Fireplace Centres plc
Pendle House
Phoenix Way
Burnley
Lancashire BB11 5SX

Card Line Greetings Ltd
Unit 4–5, Hale Trading Estate
Lower Church Lane
Tipton
West Midlands DY4 7PQ

Cash Generator
113 Bradshawgate
Bolton
BL1 1QD

Cheque Converters
11–13 Limes Court
Conduit Lane
Hoddesdon
Hertfordshire EN11 8EP

Choices Video Plus
The Home Entertainment
Corporation plc
19–24 Manesty Road
Orton
Southgate
Peterborough PE2 6UP

CNA Executive Search
Gordon Court
Lockington Hall
Lockington
Derby DE74 2RH

Colneis Marketing Ltd
York House
2–4 York Road
Felixstowe
Suffolk IP11 7QQ

Drinkmaster Ltd
Plymouth Road
Liskeard
Cornwall PL14 3PG

Dublcheck
Padeswood Hall
Padeswood
Mold
Clwyd CH7 4JF

Eismann International Ltd
Margarethe House
Eismann Way
Phoenix Park Industrial Estate
Corby
Northamptonshire NN17 1ZB

Expense Reduction Analysts
60 Albert Court
Prince Consort Road
London SW7

Fastrack Parcels Ltd
Veasey Close
Attleborough Fields
Nuneaton CV11 6RX

Fastsigns
36 High Street
New Malden
Surrey KT3 4HE

Fix-a-Chip Ltd
The Car Smart Centre
Vermont
Washington
Tyne & Wear NE37 2AX

Formative Fun
The Old School House
Gundry Lane
Bridport
Dorset DT6 3RL

Franchise Development Services
Rouen House
Rouen Road
Norwich NR1 1RB

Fresh Connection
166 Bute Street Mall
Arndale Centre
Luton LU1 2TL

Future Training & Recruitment Centres Ltd
The Old Mill
Northgrove Road
Hawkhurst
Kent TN18 4AP

Garage Door Associates Ltd
Unit 5
Meadow Brook Industrial
Centre
Maxwell Way
Crawley
West Sussex RH10 2SA

Hays Apollo Despatch
Apollo House
28–30 Hoxton Square
London N1 6NN

**Helen O'Grady's Children's
Drama Academy**
Gerenne House
Rue de la Cache
St Sampson's
Guernsey GY2 4AF

Instant Image Group Ltd
12 Duke's Court
Bognor Road
Chichester
West Sussex PO19 2FX

Jani-King
150 London Road
Kingston-upon-Thames
Surrey KT2 6QL

Leading Agencies
Spadesbourne House
184 Worcester Road
Bromsgrove
Worcestershire B61 7AZ

Martin & Co
6–8 Union Street
Yeovil BA20 1PQ

Master Brew
Beverages House
7 Ember Centre
Hersham Trading Estate
Hersham
Surrey KT12 3BT

Merryweathers
Larwood House
Whitecross
Guiseley LS20 8LZ

Nescafe Coffee House
Beverages Division
St George's House
Croydon
Surrey CR9 1NR

Nippers
Mansers
Nizels Lane
Hildenborough
Kent TN11 8NX

O'Brien's Irish Sandwich Bars
22 South Williams Street
Dublin 2

Oscar Pet Foods
Bannister Hall Mill
Higher Walton
Preston
Lancashire PR5 4DB

Priority Management
Oakwood
Spa Road
Melksham
Wiltshire SN12 7TA

Re-Nu
68 Nuffield Road
Nuffield Industrial Estate
Poole
Dorset BH17 0RS

**Rosemary Conley Diet &
Fitness Clubs Ltd**
Quorn House
Meeting Street
Quorn
Loughborough
Leicestershire LE12 8EX

Select Appointments plc
Ziggurat
Grosvenor Road
St Albans
Hertfordshire AL1 3HW

Sevenoaks Sound & Vision
109–113 London Road
Sevenoaks, Kent TN13 1BH

Sinclair Collis
Lower Walsall Street
Wolverhampton
West Midlands WV1 2ES

Snack in the Box
Dunbeath Lodge
3 Easter Road
Havant
Hants PO9 2JE

Stagecoach Theatre Arts
The Courthouse
Elm Grove
Walton-on-Thames
Surrey KT12 1LH

Stainbusters Ltd
15 Windmill Avenue
Woolpit Business Park
Bury St Edmunds
Suffolk IP30 9UP

Status Hydraulics
Status House
Cambrian Business Park
Queens Lane
Mold Flintshire CH7 1XB

Stumpbusters
PO Box 1064
Maidenhead
Berkshire SL6 6AS

Uniglobe (Great Britain &
Ireland)
Parkside
4 Calverley Park Gardens
Tunbridge Wells
Kent TN1 2JN

Ventrolla Ltd
11 Hornbeam Square South
South Harrogate
North Yorkshire HG2 8NB

VIP Bin Cleaning Ltd
VIP House
Unit 5 Frensham Road
Sweet Briar Business Park
Norwich NR3 2BT

**Worldwide Refinishing
Systems**
Spectrum House
Lower Oakham Way
Oakham Business Park
Mansfield
Nottinghamshire NG18 5BY

PROVISIONAL LISTING

Provisional listing is available for those companies developing their franchise concept and who are taking accredited professional advice on its structure.

Alliance Preservation
Northgate House
St Mary's Place
Newcastle-upon-Tyne
NE1 7PN

Apache
La Route de St Aubin
St Helier
Jersey
Channel Islands JE2 3SG

Aquaid
3A Metcalfe Road
Cambridge CB3 9EY

AWG Windscreens
Unit 4
Sheppards Business Park
Norwich Road
Lenwade
Norwich NR9 5SH

Barrett & Coe
Weavers House
Mounter Gate
Norwich NR1 1PY

BB's Coffee Muffins
RFG House
Brent Way
Brentford
Middlesex TW8 8FS

Bombolini's
16 Lawnmoor Road
Glasgow G5 0UL

Bounders
Unit 6, Barnwell Business Park
Barnwell Drive
Cambridge CB5 8UX

Candy Cottage
339A Harrogate Road
Bradford
Yorkshire BD2 3TF

Chips Away International Ltd
Breakspear House
Cave Road
Brough
N. Humberside HU15 1HL

City Info (UK) Ltd
First Floor
International House
World Trade Centre
1 St Katherine's Way
London E1 9UN

Computer Gym
The Courtyard
27A High Street
Thames Ditton
Surrey KT7 0SD

Dancia International
8 Western Street
Brighton
BN1 2PG

D'Vine Wine
B1001 Bay Street, Suite 3502
Toronto
Ontario
Canada M5S 3A6

Dix-Neuf
16 Glategny Esplanade
St Peter Port
Guernsey
Channel Islands GY1 1WN

Donut Magic
RFG House, Brent Way
Brentford
Middlesex TW8 8ES

Drivernet
6th Floor World Trade Centre
Exchange Quay
Manchester M5 3EJ

Dry Cleaning Plus
Churchill Business Centre
2 Sopwith Crescent
Wickford Business Park
Wickford
Essex SS11 8YU

Elite Introductions
Astor House
Lichfield Road
Four Oaks
Sutton Coldfield B74 2UG

Express Despatch
Sterling House
97 Lichfield Street
Tamworth B79 7QF

Felicity Hat Hire
2 Howick Park Avenue
Penwortham
Preston PR1 0LS

Filtafry
15 Macon Court
Macon Way
Crewe
Cheshire CW1 6WE

Floor Coverings International
High Quality House
Sandbeck Way
Wetherby LS22 7DN

Four in One
Port Downie
Cameron
Falkirk FK1 4QZ

Freedom Maintenance Ltd
Freedom House
Bradford Road, Tingley
Wakefield

Futurekids
21 Gloucester Road
London SW7 4PL

Gas-Elec
Brooklyn House
Money Lane
The Green
West Drayton UB7 7PQ

Getifix (UK) Ltd
Victoria Industrial Estate
14 Victoria Way
Burgess Hill
West Sussex RH15 9NF

Handwash, The
751–755 Ashton Old Road
Openshaw
Manchester M11 2HB

Hire Intelligence
35 Maida Vale
London W9 1TP

Kenco
St George's House
Bayshill Road
Cheltenham
Gloucestershire GL50 3AE

Kendlebell
Carolyn House
22–26 Dingwall Road
Croydon
Surrey CR0 9XF

Lynx Courier Services
1 St George's Street
Bermuda Industrial Estate
Nuneaton
Warwickshire CV10 7JS

Mail Boxes Etc
10 Suffolk House
George Street
Croydon CR0 1PE

Nationwide Auto Service
Finelist Group plc
Regal House
Birmingham Road
Stratford-upon-Avon
Warwickshire CV37 0BN

Paint Technik
PO Box 5066
Leighton Buzzard
Bedfordshire LU7 7YS

Photo-Arts
Barnfield Trading Estate
Ramsay Road
Tipton
West Midlands DY4 9DU

Regency Introductions
Three Spires House
16A Bird Street
Lichfield
Staffordshire WS13 6PR

Ripples
Chelsea House
London Road
Bath BA1 6DB

Roaduser
Maccess
Spen Lane
Cleckheaton
West Yorkshire BD19 4PG

Sales Recruitment Network
42 Smithy Close
Brindle
Chorley
Lancashire PR6 8NW

Salon Services
82–90 Kelvin Avenue
Hillington
Glasgow G52 4LT

Speed Couriers
Cromwell House
3 Meadow Lane
St Ives
Cambridgeshire PE17 4LG

Surface Doctor
14 Metro Centre
Springfield Road
Hayes
Middlesex UB4 0LE

Swisher
9 Churchill Court
33 Palmerston Road
Bournemouth BH1 4HN

Tapas Tree
Progress House
Castlefields Lane
Bingley DB16 2AB

TaxAssist Direct Ltd
TaxAssist House
58 Thorpe Road
Norwich NR1 1RY

Temples
Suite 1
12 Bank Street
Norwich NR2 4SE

Trophy
11–12 Market Place
Faringdon
Oxfordshire SN7 7HP

Urban Planters
202 Pasture Lane
Bradford
West Yorkshire BD7 2SE

User 2
Unit 10
Greencroft Industrial Park
Annfield Plain
Co. Durham DH9 7YB

15 Useful Organisations and Publications

OVERSEAS SERVICES

The British Franchise Association's Overseas Service, launched in 1991, is a listing of all those individuals and organisations outside the UK who have an interest in UK franchising, whether as a franchisor looking to operate in the UK or looking to find a UK partner; or as a professional adviser interested in helping UK companies to extend their operations overseas.

The Overseas Service is open to any company who wants to subscribe. The lists below indicate which subscribers are members or associates of their own National Franchise Association.

Consultants

David Acheson Partnership
14 Royena Place
Marcus Beach
Queensland 4573
Tel: 010 61 074 481 774
Fax: 010 61 074 481 775
(Member of Australia/NZ
Franchise Association)

**Franchise Development
Services (Middle East)**
PO Box 221
Jeddah 21411
Saudi Arabia
Tel: 00 996 2 651 5123
Fax: 00 996 2 651 5123

National and international franchise associations

Franchisors Association of Australia
Unit 9, 2–6 Hubter Street
Paramatta NSW 2150
Australia

Austrian Franchise Association*
Bayerhamerstrasse 12
1st Floor
5020 Salzburg
Austria

Belgian Franchise Federation*
Bd de L'Humantie 116/22
1070 Brussels
Belgium

Brazilian Franchise Association
Ave Prof. Ascendino Reis
1548 Indianpolis
Sao Paulo
Brazil CEP 04027 000

British Franchise Association*
Thames View
Newtown Road
Henley-on-Thames
Oxon RG9 1HG

Canadian Franchise Association
5045 Orbitor Drive
Building 12, Unit 210
Mississauga
Ontario
Canada L4W 4Y4

Czech Franchise Association*
Rytirska 18–20
110 00 Prag 1
Czech Republic

Danish Franchise Assocation*
Maglebjergvej 5 B-D
DK-2800 Lyngby
Denmark

European Franchise Federation*
Bd de L'Humantie 116/22
1070 Brussels
Belgium

Finnish Franchise Association*
PL 39
08501 Lohja
Finland

French Franchise Association*
60 rue la Boetie
75008 Paris
France

**German Franchise
Association***
Paul-Heyse-Strasse 33–35
Munich 80336
Germany

**Hong Kong Franchise
Association**
22/F United Centre
95 Queensway
Hong Kong

**Hungarian Franchise
Association***
c/o DASY
PO Box 446
Budapest H-1536

**International Franchise
Association**
1350 New York Avenue NW
#900
Washington DC 20005
USA

Irish Franchise Association
13 Frankfield Terrace
Summerhill South
Cork
Republic of Ireland

Israel Franchise Association
Corex Building
Maskit Street
Herzlia Pituach 46733
Israel

**Italian Franchising
Association***
Corso di Porto Nuova 3
20121 Milan
Italy

**Franchise Association of
Greece***
24 Raidestou Street
GR 171 22
Nea Smyrni
Greece

**Japanese Franchise
Association**
Elsa Building 602
3–13–12 Rippongi
Minato-ku
Tokyo
Japan

**Mexican Franchise
Association**
Insurgentes Sur 1783 No 303
Colinia Guadeloupe Inn
Mexico City 01020
Mexico

**Netherlands Franchise
Association***
Boomberglaan
1217 RR Hilversum
The Netherlands

**Norwegian Franchise
Association**
Pstboks 2483 Solli
Oslo 2 0202
Norway

Polish Franchise Association*
1 Szpitalna Street
II Floor Room 5
00–02-Warsaw
Poland

**Portuguese Franchise
Association***
Rua Castilho 14
1200 Lisbon
Portugal

**Romanian Franchise
Association***
Bd Aviatorilor 86
Sector 1
Bucharest
Romania

**Franchise Association of
Southern Africa**
PO Box 31708
2017 Braamfontein
Republic of South Africa

**Spanish Franchise
Association***
Avda de la Ferias s/n
Apdo 476
46080 Valencia
Spain

**Swedish Franchise
Association***
PB 5512
s-114 85 Stockholm
Sweden

Swiss Franchise Association*
Lowenstrasse 11 Postfach
8039 Zurich
Switzerland

Turkish Franchise Association
Sclimc Hatun Camii Sokak
Ozlen Apt No 13/4
Gumussuyu
Istanbul
Turkey

**Yugoslav Franchise
Association***
Mokranjceva 28
2100 Novi Sad
Yugoslavia

BFA Affiliate Listing
Bankers

Barclays Bank plc
Franchise Department
Swift House
PO Box 120
Longwood Close
Westwood Business Park
Coventry CV4 8JN
Tel: 01203 534433
Contact: Mr R J Cracknell
www.barclays.co.uk

*Member of European Franchise
Federation

221

Lloyds Bank plc
Retail Banking UKRB
PO Box 112
Canon's Way
Bristol BS99 7LB
Tel: 0117 943 3410
Contact: Mr M S Hatcliffe
www.lloydsbank.co.uk/franchis/

Midland Bank plc
Franchise Unit
10 Lower Thames Street
London EC3R 6AE
Tel: 0171 260 6783
Contact: Mrs C Hayes
www.midlandbank.co.uk

NatWest UK
Retail Banking Services –
Franchise Section
Level 10, Drapers Gardens
12 Throgmorton Avenue
London EC2N 2DL
Tel: 0171 920 5966
Contact: Mr P D Stern
www.natwest.co.uk

The Royal Bank of Scotland plc
Franchise and Licensing
Department
PO Box 31
42 St Andrew Square
Edinburgh EH2 2YE
Tel: 0131 556 8555
Contact: Mr G Rose
www.rbs.co.uk/franchise/

Business schools, research centres and training providers

Cranfield School of Management
Cranfield
Bedfordshire
MK43 0AL
Contact: Mr C Barrow

Franchise and Training Centre
25 New Street Square
London EC4A 3LN
Tel: 0171 917 9824
Contact: Mr B Duckett

The Franchise Training Centre
212 Piccadilly
London W1V 9LD
Tel: 0171 917 2837
Contact: Mr B Duckett

University of Westminster
35 Marylebone Road
London NW1 5LS
Tel: 0171 911 5000
Contact: Prof. J Stanworth

Chartered accountants

Beresfords
Castle House
Castle Hill Avenue
Folkestone
Kent CT20 2TQ
Tel: 01303 850992
Fax: 01303 850979
Contact: Mr T C Hindle

Fraser Russell
Albany House
128 Station Road
Redhill
Surrey RH1 1ET
Tel: 01737 765451
Contact: Mr R J Mitchell

Kidsons Impey
Carlton House
31–34 Railway Street
Chelmsford
Essex CM1 1NJ
Tel: 01245 269595
Contact: Mr D V Collins

Levy Gee
66 Wigmore Street
London W1H 0HQ
Tel: 0171 467 4000
Contact: Mr J Synett

Pannell Kerr Forster
78 Carlton Place
Glasgow G5 9TH
Tel: 0141 429 5900
Contact: Mr E Fraser

Rees Pollock
7 Pilgrim Street
London EC4V 6DR
Tel: 0171 329 6404
Contact: Mr W A Pollock

Exhibition organisers

CDFEX
78 Carlton Place
Glasgow G5 9TH
Tel: 0141 429 5900
Contact: Mr J Sellyn

CII
Carlton Plaza
11 Upper Richmond Road
Putney
London SW15 2TJ
Tel: 0181 785 2288
Contact: Mr M J Stride

Miller Freeman UK Ltd
630 Chiswick High Road
London W4 5BG
Tel: 0181 742 2828
Contact: Mr K Brinkley

Factors

Griffin Credit Services Ltd
Griffin House
21 Farncombe Road
Worthing
West Sussex BN11 2BW
Tel: 01903 205181
Fax: 01903 214101
Contact: Mr B J Cooper

**The Factors and Discounters
Association**
Administration Office
2nd Floor Boston House
The Little Green
Richmond
Surrey TW9 1QE
Tel: 0181 332 9955
Fax: 0181 332 2585

Franchise consultants

Baker Tilley
2 Bloomsbury Street
London WC1B 3ST
Tel: 0171 413 5212
Contact: Mr T Mundella

**BDO Stoy Hayward
Management Consultants**
8 Baker Street
London W1M 1DA
Tel: 0171 486 5888
Contact: Mr Max McHardy
www.bdo.co.uk

CFM Consulting
Briarwood House
Langhurst Road
Woldingham
Surrey CR3 7HF
Tel: 01883 653178
Contact: M Taube

**Franchise & Marketing
Management Ltd (FMM)**
46–48 Thornhill Road
Streetly
Sutton Coldfield
West Midlands B74 3EH
Tel: 0121 353 0031/2
Contact: Mr M Matthews

**Franchise Development
Services**
Surrey House
56 Surrey Street
Norwich NR1 3FD
Tel: 01603 620301
Contact: Mr D A Mayers

**Franchise Development
Services** (Midlands)
4200 Waterside Centre
Solihull Parkway
Birmingham Business Park
Birmingham B37 7YN
Tel: 0121 717 4717
Contact: Mr I Martin

Franchise Development Services (Southern)
Maple Grove
Bradfield
Reading
Berks RG7 6DH
Tel: 01189 745115
Contact: Mr G Patterson

Franchise Development Services (London)
10 Greenaway Gardens
London NW3 7DJ
Tel: 0171 794 6356
Contact: Mr L H Levi

Horwath Franchising
25 New Street Square
London EC4A 3LN
Tel: 0171 917 9824
Contact: Mr B Duckett

Peter Williams
40 Newquay Close
Nuneaton
Warwickshire CV11 6FH
Tel: 01203 329260
Contact: Mr P Williams

The Franchise and Licensing Division (England)
New Garden House
78 Hatton Garden
London EC1N 8JA
Tel: 0171 831 7393
Contact: Ms Nina Moran
www.pkf.com/uk/formatf

The Franchise and Licensing Division (Scotland)
78 Carlton Place
Glasgow G5 9TH
Tel: 0141 429 5900
Contact: Mr Euan Fraser
www.pkf.com/uk/formatf

The Franchise Company
Ashburn House
84 Grange Road
Darlington
Co Durham DL1 5NP
Tel: 01325 251455
Fax: 01323 251466
e-mail:
franchise/co@virgin.net
freespace.virgin.net/franchise.
co/franch.htm

Franchise manual publishing consultants

Manual Writers International
49 Bradmore
Park Road
London W6 0DT
Tel: 07000 315750
Contact: Mrs P Hopkinson
www.british-franchise.
org.uk/manual–writers/

Insurance brokers

Tolsen
148 King Street
London W6 0QU
Tel: 0181 741 8361
Contact: Mr D Perfect

Media, communications and publications

Business Franchise Magazine
630 Chiswick High Road
London W4 5BG
Tel: 01925 724326
Contact: Mrs L Lister

Franchise World
James House
37 Nottingham Road
London SW17 7EA
Tel: 0181 767 1371
Contact: Mr Robert Riding

The Express Business Plus
(Official Newspaper to the BFA)
Ludgate House
245 Blackfriars Road
London SE1 9UX
Tel: 0171 928 8000
Contact: Mr M Nugent

The Franchise Magazine
Rouen House
Rouen Road
Norwich NR1 1RB
Tel: 01603 620301
Contact: Dr D R Chaplin

Patent and trade mark attorneys

Ladas & Parry
52–54 High Holborn
London WC1V 6RR
Tel: 0171 242 5566
Contact: Mr I C Baillie
New York Bar & UK Chart.
Patent and Trade Mark Agent

Solicitors

Addleshaw Booth & Co
Dennis House
Marsden Street
Manchester M2 1JD
Tel: 0161 832 5994
Contact: Mr G Lindrup

Beveridge Ross & Prevezer
10–11 New Street
London EC2M 4TP
Tel: 0171 626 1533
Contact: Mr J Cohen &
Mr R Levitt

Biggart Baillie & Gifford
Dalmore House
310 St Vincent Street
Glasgow G2 5QR
Tel: 0141 228 8000
Contact: Mr C Miller

Brodies
15 Atholl Crescent
Edinburgh EH3 8HA
Tel: 0131 228 3777
Contact: Mr J C A Voge

Burstows
8 Ifield Road
Crawley
West Sussex RH11 7YY
Tel: 01293 603603
Fax: 01293 603666
Contact: Mrs C Armitage

Chambers & Co
Jonathan Scott Hall
Thorpe Road
Norwich NR1 1UH
Tel: 01603 616155
Contact: Mr J Chambers

Clairmonts
9 Clairmont Gardens
Glasgow G3 7LW
Tel: 0141 226 3020
Contact: Mr D S Kaye

David Bigmore & Co
36 Whitefriars Street
London EC4Y 8BH
Tel: 0171 583 2277
Contact: Mr D Bigmore (BFA
Legal Committee)

Eversheds
Holland Court
The Close
Norwich NR1 4DX
Tel: 01603 272727
Contact: Mr M Bayliss

Eversheds
Cloth Court Hall
Infirmary Street
Leeds LS1 2JB
Tel: 0113 243 0391
Contact: Mr P Heatherington

Eversheds
Fitzalan House
Fitzalan Road
Cardiff CF2 1XZ
Tel: 01222 471147
Contact: Mrs H McNabb

Eversheds
11–12 Queen Square
Bristol BS1 4NT
Tel: 0117 929 9555
Contact: Mr P Sampson

Eversheds
1 Royal Standard Place
Nottingham NG1 6FZ
Tel: 0115 950 7000
Contact: Mr M Knibbs

Eversheds
10 Newhall Street
Birmingham B3 3LX
Tel: 0121 233 2001
Contact: Mr P Manford

Eversheds
Sun Alliance House
35 Mosley Street
Newcastle-upon-Tyne
NE1 1XX
Tel: 0191 261 1661
Fax: 0191 261 8267
Contact: Mr P Heatherington

Eversheds
Senator House
85 Queen Victoria Street
London EC4V 4JL
Tel: 0171 919 4500
Contact: Mr M Mendelsohn
(BFA Legal Committee)

Field Fisher Waterhouse
41 Vine Street
London EC3N 2AA
Tel: 0171 481 4841
Contact: Mr M Abell (BFA
Legal Committee)

Hammond Suddards
16 John Dalton Street
Manchester M60 8HS
Tel: 0161 830 5000
Contact: Mrs P Cowie
e-mail: Pauline.Cowie
@HammondSuddards.co.uk

Hammond Suddards
7 Devonshire Gardens
London EC2M 4YH
Tel: 0171 655 1000
Contact: Mrs P Cowie
e-mail: Pauline.Cowie
@HammondSuddards.co.uk

JST Mackintosh
Colonial Chambers
Temple Street
Liverpool L2 5RH
Tel: 0151 282 2828
Contact: Mr G Howard Jones

Keeble Hawson Moorhouse
(Solicitors)
Protection House
16–17 East Parade
Leeds LS1 2BR
Tel: 0113 244 3121
Contact: Mr H D McKillip

Lawrence Tucketts
Bush House
72 Prince Street
Bristol BS99 7JZ
Tel: 0117 929 5295
Contact: Mr R M Staunton

Leathes Prior
74 The Close
Norwich
Norfolk NR1 4DR
Tel: 01603 610911
Contact: Mr R J Chadd
e-mail:
jc.leathes@btinternet.com

Levy & Macrae
266 St Vincent Street
Glasgow G2 5RL
Tel: 0141 307 2311
Contact: Mr A Caplan

Maclay Murray & Spens
151 St Vincent Street
Glasgow G2 5NJ
Tel: 0141 248 5011
Contact: Ms M Burnside

Mundays
Crown House
Church Road
Glaygate
Esher KT10 0LP
Tel: 01372 467272
Contact: Mr M Ishani (BFA
Legal Committee)
www.Ids.co.uk/franchise/legal/
mundays

Nina Moran Watson
New Garden House
78 Hatton Garden
London EC1N 8JA
Tel: 0171 831 7393
Contact: Ms Nina Moran
Watson

Osbourne Clarke
50 Queen Charlotte Street
Bristol BS1 4HE
Tel: 0117 923 0220
Contact: Mr A Braithwaite

Owen White
Senate House
62–70 Bath Road
Slough
Berkshire SL1 3SR
Tel: 01753 536846
Contact: Mr A Bates (Legal
Adviser to the BFA)

Parker Bullen
45 Castle Street
Salisbury
Wilts SP1 3SS
Tel: 01722 412000
Fax: 01722 411822
Contact: Mr M Iello

Paul K Nolan & Co
135 Upper Lisburn Road
Belfast BT10 0LH
Tel: 01232 301933
Contact: Mr P Nolan

Peters & Peters
2 Harewood Place
Hanover Square
London W1R 9HB
Tel: 0171 629 7991
Contact: Mr R Cannon (BFA
Legal Committee)

Pinsent Curis
3 Colmore Circus
Birmingham B4 6BH
Tel: 0121 200 1050
Contact: Mr J Pratt

Shadbolt & Co
Chatham Court
Lesbourne
Reigate
Surrey RH2 7LD
Tel: 01737 226277
Contact: Mr A J Trotter

Sherwin Oliver
New Hampshire Court
St Paul's Road
Portsmouth PO5 4JT
Tel: 01705 832200
Contact: Mr G Sturgess

Sylvester Amiel Lewin & Horne
Pearl Assurance House
319 Ballards Lane
London N12 8LY
Tel: 0171 446 4000
Contact: Mr J Horne

Taylor Johnson Garrett
Carmelite
50 Victoria Embankment
Blackfriars
London EC4Y 0DX
Tel: 0171 353 1234
Contact: Mr C Lloyd

Thomas Eggar Church Adams
Fulwood House
Fulwood Place
London WC1V 6HR
Tel: 0171 242 0841
Contact: Mr R Brown

Wragge & Co
55 Colmore Row
Birmingham B3 2AS
Tel: 0121 233 1000
Contact: Mr G D Harris

Wright Johnston & Mackenzie
12 St Vincent Place
Glasgow
G1 2EQ
Tel: 0141 248 3434
Contact: Mr K McCracken

Other important organisations

British Insurance and Investment Brokers Association
BIIBA House
14 Bevis Marks
London EC3A 7NT
Tel: 0171 623 9043
Can recommend appropriate local brokers.

The Chartered Association of Certified Accountants
29 Lincoln's Inn Fields
London WC2A 3EE
Tel: 0171 242 6855

The Chartered Institute of Management Accountants
63 Portland Place
London W1N 4AB
Tel: 0171 637 2311

Companies Registration Office
Keeps records of all limited companies. For England and Wales these records are kept at:
London Search Room
55 City Road
London EC1Y 1BB
Tel: 0171 253 9393

Crown Way
Maindy
Cardiff CF4 3UZ
Tel: 01222 388588
Web site: http//www.
companies-house.gov.uk

and for Scotland:
Companies House
37 Castle Terrace
Edinburgh EH1 2EB
Tel: 0131 535 5800

Extel
Fitzroy House
13–17 Epworth Street
London EC2A 4DL
Tel: 0171 251 3333

Corporation of Insurance and Financial Advisors (CIFA)
174 High Street
Guildford
Surrey GU1 3HW
Tel: 01483 539121
For commercial mortgages.

Department of Trade and Industry
1–19 Victoria Street
London SW1H 0GT
Tel: 0171 215 7877
Web site: http//www.dti.gov.uk

Institute of Chartered Accountants in England and Wales
PO Box 433
Chartered Accountants Hall
Moorgate Place
London EC2P 2BJ
Tel: 0171 920 8100
Web site:
http://www.icaew.co.uk

The Institute of Chartered Accountants of Scotland
27 Queen Street
Edinburgh EH2 1LA
Tel: 0131 225 5673
Web site:
http://www.kas.org.uk

The National Federation of Self-Employed and Small Businesses
2 Catherine Place
Westminster
London SW1E 6HF
Tel: 0171 928 9272
and

32 Orchard Road
Lytham St Annes
Lancashire FY8 1NY
Tel: 01253 720911

Further reading from Kogan Page

Business Growth Handbook
*Colin Barrow, Robert Brown and
Liz Clarke* (Kogan Page),
price £15.99 paperback.*

Business Plan Workbook
*Colin Barrow, Paul Barrow and
Robert Brown* 3rd edition 1998
(Kogan Page), price £9.99
paperback.

**Financial Management for the
Small Business**
The Daily Telegraph Guide,
Colin Barrow, 4th edition 1998
(Kogan Page), price £9.99
paperback.

Working for Yourself
The Daily Telegraph Guide,
Godfrey Golzen, 16th edition
1995 (Kogan Page), price £9.99
paperback.

---

*For further information on Kogan Page publications tel: 0171 278 0433; Web site:
www.kogan-page.co.uk

Index

Index of Advertisers

Visit Kogan Page on-line

Comprehensive information on
Kogan Page titles

Features include

- complete catalogue listings,
  including book reviews and
  descriptions

- special monthly promotions

- information on NEW titles and
  BESTSELLING titles

- a secure shopping basket facility
  for on-line ordering

PLUS everything you need to know
about KOGAN PAGE

http://www.kogan-page.co.uk